LUMEN CHRISTI

OS JUSTI STUDIES IN CATHOLIC TRADITION
General Editor: Peter A. Kwasniewski

Lumen Christi

DEFENDING THE USE
OF THE
PRE-1955 ROMAN RITE

BY A BENEDICTINE OBLATE

Foreword by Peter Kwasniewski

OS JUSTI
PRESS

Os Justi Press
P.O. Box 21814
Lincoln, NE 68542
www.osjustipress.com

Send inquiries to
info@osjustipress.com

ISBN 978-1-965303-40-5 (paperback)
ISBN 978-1-965303-39-9 (hardcover)
ISBN 978-1-965303-41-2 (ebook)

Book design by Michael Schrauzer
Cover photograph by Juliana Lamb

The legacy of the Lord, the Mass is the sun of our lives and our treasure. We love it due to the fact that it is substantially and principally of the Lord's [own] institution. But we love it also as the Church, to which Jesus entrusted its celebration, has transmitted it to us down through the centuries by means of the various liturgical traditions — because the prayers and rites developed through the centuries in order to explain and manifest before the eyes of the entire Church the unfathomable riches of the essential rite bequeathed by the Lord....

We cannot in any way forswear a heritage slowly built by the Faith of our fathers, their burning devotion, and the theological reflection around the sacrament of the Passion of the Lord. In contact with the Mass of Saint Pius V — in which we also contemplate the purest masterpiece of Western civilization, hierarchical as well as sacral — our souls lift up and our hearts expand, while our minds taste the most authentic Eucharistic doctrine. This is why we wish to understand and love, at all times more, the Traditional Mass, our treasure, and we will not cease to defend and advance it.

— Abbé Franck Marie Quoëx

CONTENTS

FOREWORD

THERE WAS A TIME, NOT SO LONG AGO, when the discovery of the Church's ancient liturgy was a moment of unexpected wonder for many. Curious souls might find themselves in a Low or Solemn Mass, entirely unaware of what awaited. What they found was not only ancient ceremonies, but an awakening: the realization that the Church's liturgy had once been something wholly different from the simplified ceremonies they had hitherto known. This book, *Lumen Christi*, stands as both a testimony to that awakening and a guide for those still walking that same path.

The traditional Mass is not an isolated jewel. Those who encounter the Mass soon discover the older rites of baptism, marriage, ordination, and blessings. They soon learn of the Divine Office, which was once the daily heartbeat of clergy and laity alike. Piece by piece, they come to understand that the Roman rite, once the serene inheritance of countless saints, was not abruptly overturned in the late 1960s; instead, it was subjected to decades of slow dismantling. By the time the Council was convened, much of the damage had already been done.

The story of rupture did not begin with Vatican II; it began much earlier. *Lumen Christi* does not shy away from this uncomfortable truth. Among the most significant turning points was the imposition of the reformed Holy Week in 1955 under Pope Pius XII. This was no gentle pruning, but a deliberate reshaping of ancient ceremonies to fit the mind of modern man. Pitched as a "restoration," these reforms were in fact a rupture — an attempt to reimagine and improve upon the past rather than receiving it humbly.

To "restore" and to "simplify" may sound innocent, but these impulses are thoroughly modern and foreign to the very spirit of the Roman rite. Authentic liturgical development never came from panels of experts wielding historical tools. It emerged from the living faith of the Church, slowly refined in its expressions over the course of centuries. *Lumen Christi* rightly highlights the work of the 1948 Liturgical Commission — a body that operated largely in secret, but with full papal backing, whose efforts ultimately treated the inherited rites of the Church not as treasures to be safeguarded, but as raw materials for reconstruction.

The mentality that "continuity is whatever authority declares it to be" is one of the great errors of our age. Continuity is not something that can be legislated into existence; it is a reality, visible in the organic development of texts, gestures, and prayers across centuries. To claim that a radically altered rite is the same as its predecessor simply because a competent authority says so is to fall into the error of nominalism — the idea that names define reality, rather than reality determining names.

What this book calls for is not nostalgia but intellectual honesty and historical clarity. The classical Roman rite (including its ancient Holy Week, its traditional calendar, and its undiminished prayers) is not a museum piece; it is the Church's living liturgy, shaped by saints and hallowed by time. It is this authentic inheritance — not the compromised text of 1962, still bearing the wounds of earlier reforms, and anticipating further wounds to come — that the faithful are increasingly coming to recognize as their birthright. To defend this rite is not to reject authority but to remind authority of its limits. No pope, no council, and no commission possesses the power to erase the inheritance of the Church. What was sacred to our forefathers remains sacred for us today. This is the conviction that animates the pages of *Lumen Christi*. Its learned author defends not only a particular liturgical form but the very principle of tradition itself — that what has been received and handed down possesses a unique authority, independent of the whims of any given age.

In the end, our task is simple: to emerge from the cave of modern liturgical innovations into the full light of tradition. This book offers a roadmap for that journey. May it aid both clergy and laity alike in rediscovering the luminous beauty of the classical Roman Rite, the *Lumen Christi* that no darkness can overcome.

Peter A. Kwasniewski

June 11, 2025

Ember Wednesday in the Octave of Pentecost

ACKNOWLEDGMENTS

HIS WORK WOULD NOT HAVE BEEN POS-
sible without the invaluable assistance of Dr. Peter
Kwasniewski, whose generosity in offering his time
and expertise, as well as his willingness to promote
the work, has been of immense benefit throughout the process
of writing and editing. His tireless efforts to advocate for the
restoration of the Roman rite in its classical form, combined
with his extensive published works, have significantly contributed
to the growing interest in the authentic traditional liturgy. It is
within this context of renewed interest that the necessity for the
present book has arisen.

Special acknowledgement must also be given to Anthony
Jones and a traditional priest in good standing who must remain
unnamed. Their thorough and insightful editorial contributions
have been essential in ensuring the accuracy and reliability of
the text. Gratitude is especially due to Mr. Jones, whose careful
work enhanced the text's clarity and academic rigor.

Further thanks must be extended to Dr. Ilya A. Kotlyar, whose
meticulous work on the sections concerning canon law ensured
that these passages are both precise and in full accordance with
the relevant legal standards.

I would also like to express my sincere gratitude to my fel-
low parishioners for their constant support and encouragement
throughout the development of this work. Finally, my deepest
thanks go to my wife, Elisa, whose unwavering patience, love,
and support have made this work possible.

A Benedictine Oblate
March 19, 2025
Feast of St. Joseph, Spouse of the Blessed Virgin Mary

1

Tradition and Liturgy

ROM THE BEGINNING OF THE VISIBLE existence of the Church on earth, the liturgy has been held in high esteem. Since it has always been believed that the Holy Sacrifice of the Mass is Calvary made present, the Church has deemed it worthy of reverence and protection. Countless saints and martyrs shed their blood and endured persecution to defend the Mass and the Faith it embodies from those who tried to destroy and undermine it. It is with this in mind that we ought to attend and study the liturgy with the sincerest faith and humility. It is impossible to separate the Mass from tradition. It is only by tradition that the Mass reaches us. Our fathers in the Faith held this Mass dear to themselves, for it is the pinnacle of our religion. This is why so many of them would rather attend the Mass, Offices, and sacraments than enjoy the vanities of this temporary world. It is solely by their love and devotion to the Mass, in times of freedom and of persecution, that we have the privilege of attending the sacrifice to this day.

Some say that the Mass of our ancestors is the same as the Mass we see in our day. This is true — but only to an extent. It is by the work of the Holy Ghost in the Church that the Mass developed over time. The Mass of the Fathers of the Church is still recognizable to those who attend the classical Roman rite. Take, for instance, the *Ordo Romanus Primus*, which dates from somewhere between the sixth and eighth centuries in Rome: one sees a striking similarity with the Roman rite of Mass codified after Trent. The structure of the Mass, the vestments, the processions, the offertory, the Canon, and the Communion rite are almost identical to those of the classical Roman rite. One can even hear the same chants, such as the Kyrie, the Gloria, the Sanctus, and the Ite missa est. Its very heart, the ancient Canon of the Mass, is the same. We know that Pope St. Gregory the Great (590–604) was the last pope (until John XXIII) to modify the text, adding the words *diesque nostros in tua pace disponas* ("and order our days in

Thy peace")[1] It has been said that the Roman clergy and faithful in those days were upset that he touched something as venerable as the *Canon Missae* already was by that time; some even said it should be a punishable offence.[2] How the times have changed.

One of the oldest maxims in the Church is attributed to Prosper of Aquitaine in the fifth century: "the law of praying establishes the law of believing," or, in its familiar abbreviation, *lex orandi, lex credendi*. It perfectly encapsulates the Church's view on tradition and liturgy. Some add *lex vivendi* to this pair, as if to say: how one must live is determined by the law of what one believes, which is determined in turn by the law of what one prays. One can deduce that

> the *lex orandi* comes first: doctrine is expressed principally in and through our inherited worship.... The liturgy is the "home" of the Faith. It is the primary canon that measures all canons, the most authoritative utterance of revelation, the primordial catechism that contains and passes on our holy religion.[3]

There is a direct correlation between what we pray and how we live. The Mass, being the central prayer of the Church, has a significant role in the way in which we live. One can see in our times how changing the law of prayer can cause havoc and destruction in the lives of many. Not that long ago, seminaries were full, as were monasteries and convents. The Church had grown and had catechized the world in the name of Christ, helping numerous souls enter into the heavenly abode. It was only in a short amount of time (so it seemed) that some churchmen and theologians lost their Catholic faith as to what the Mass truly is. No longer was it seen as the sacrifice of Calvary made present. Rather, it was seen as a communal supper meal. What was the

---

[1] Adrian Fortescue, *The Mass: A Study of the Roman Liturgy* (Longmans, Green & Co., 1914), 172. One must use this work with care, however, as it is dated in some of its scholarship. For the best recent scholarly work on the Roman Rite, see Uwe Michael Lang, *The Roman Mass: From Early Christian Origins to Tridentine Reform* (Cambridge University Press, 2022).

[2] Gregory Hesse, "Canon Lawyer on the Validity/Invalidity of the Novus Ordo Sacraments," Internet Archive, archived on June 3, 2016, at https://archive.org/details/CanonLawyerOnTheValidityInvalidityOfTheNovusOrdoSacraments.

[3] Peter Kwasniewski, *The Once and Future Roman Rite: Returning to the Traditional Latin Liturgy after Seventy Years of Exile* (TAN Books, 2022), 335.

effect of this fundamental shift, with all that accompanied it? Vocations dwindled. Devotions were thrown aside. Mass attendance significantly dropped. Traditional teachings were seen as outdated and in need of *aggiornamento*. To think that all these atrocities occurred so rapidly! How could this be? *Lex orandi, lex credendi, lex vivendi.*

The only way in which the Church can recover from the current crisis she endures is by reuniting with her past. It is only by looking at tradition that we can gain a sense of what the Church should be and what the Church has lost. No one knows when the crisis of faith will end, but we do know that the only way for the Church to survive is by tradition: with the traditional Mass, the traditional sacraments, traditional devotions, and the traditional faith.

Many today believe that the crisis in the Church can be solved only by the restoration of the traditional Latin Mass. However, it will take more than just the restoration of the Mass. One also needs the restoration of the Faith in its entirety. This includes restoring various practices such as traditional feasts and fasts, traditional penances, traditional pieties, and traditional living. The Eucharist is the spring from which all graces flow; the separation of Mass and faith is impossible. Some organizations these days celebrate the "old Mass" while maintaining a "new faith," but this simply will not work. "No man can serve two masters. For either he will hate the one and love the other: or he will sustain the one and despise the other. You cannot serve God and mammon" (Matt 6:24). Those of good faith who belong to these unfortunate organizations end up fighting for the old Mass but compromise more than they can uphold.

When one decides to embrace the authentic Roman rite, one cannot bear to see the lack of beauty and reverence elsewhere. The restoration of the true Mass to its proper place in the Church is a stepping stone for the restoration of hearts to Jesus Christ. This is the true Catholic faith that nourished the saints, the Faith for which the martyrs died. This is the motivation for the movement to restore the ancient rites of the Church: the glorification of God and the creation of saints.

The Classical Roman Rite: From 1570 Until the Twentieth Century

T IS A COMMON MISCONCEPTION TO believe that the Tridentine Mass was created at the Council of Trent. While the Council of Trent (1545–1563) did play a significant role in prompting liturgical reforms, the specific form of the Tridentine Mass was established later with the promulgation of the Roman Missal by Pope St. Pius V in 1570. The 1570 *Missale Romanum* codified the Roman rite as celebrated in the papal court, going back to Innocent III's *Ordo Missae* of the early thirteenth century, which already reflected the millennial tradition of the Roman rite and kindred uses found throughout Europe and beyond. (It bears mentioning that the Franciscans had been celebrating this form of the Roman rite since 1223 and had made it widespread in Europe.) This effort at codification was guided by the Council of Trent's desire for a unified response to the Protestant Revolt. Pius V consulted with liturgical scholars and clergy to ensure that the missal was both theologically sound and practical. The result was a uniform text designed to bring consistency to the celebration of the Mass across the diverse regions of the Church. The Council of Trent in its final session asked that the projects for a universal catechism and revised breviary and missal be brought to completion at the hands of the Roman Pontiff.[1] The *Missale Romanum* of 1570 was purely a codification of what was already familiar in the curial rite of Rome. This was chosen because the "*Missale Romanum consuetudinem Romanae Curiae* had the greatest vogue" at the time.[2] The 1474 *Missale Romanum Mediolani*, one of the complete missals published well before the Council of Trent, is practically identical to the missal canonized by Pope St. Pius V. This can readily be seen in the Propers of Mass, the *Ordo Missae*, and the

---

[1] See Session XXV, December 1563, On the Index of Books; on the Catechism, Breviary, and Missal.

[2] Josef A. Jungmann, *The Mass of the Roman Rite: Its Origins and Development (Missarum Sollemnia)*, trans. Francis A. Brunner (Benziger, 1951), 1:135.

venerable ceremonies of Holy Week. The idea of having a single book was revived at this time,[3] but in no way were the rites contained therein created.[4] The Council of Trent desired a certain standardization of liturgy that removed superfluous variations throughout the world. In creating this text, Pope St. Pius V was not creating a "new rite of Mass." He was only compiling the texts and practices of the Roman rite at that time. Similarly, Pius V allowed rites that were older than two hundred years to continue in force. This is what explains the continued presence of the Dominican rite (or, more properly, use), the rite of Lyon, and the Ambrosian rite. Although the number two hundred may initially seem arbitrary, it was chosen for two reasons: first, because two centuries prior to 1570 places one squarely *before* the period in which there arose heretical proto-reform movements that would eventually culminate in the Protestant Revolt; and second, because such a period demonstrates that the rite has long been "approved and received" in the Church, and so must be considered venerable, orthodox, and worthy. For their part, the older Roman ceremonies of Holy Week have been celebrated for *much* longer than two hundred years.

Accompanying the 1570 Missale Romanum was a decree of Pope Pius V entitled *Quo Primum*. This was one of the first decrees from the Holy See binding in perpetuity, threatening divine retribution against anyone who would add to or subtract from the liturgical

---

[3] Note that the last widespread single missal was the *Missale Plenarium* of the sixth century.

[4] It is often erroneously said that Sequences found in the missal were abolished by the Council of Trent or by Pius V. In fact, it was in uses other than that of the Roman curia that Sequences tended to proliferate; whereas the missal he promulgated already contained very few Sequences, so it was not a question of removing its existing content but, effectively, of limiting Sequences in places that chose to adopt a Roman missal that had long been reluctant to adopt new liturgical elements. Before and after the Council of Trent, only four sequences were included in the Roman Missal: those for Easter, Pentecost, Corpus Christi, and the Mass for the Dead. The gradual adoption of the curial missal led to the unintended consequence of many medieval Sequences disappearing. Some exceptions remained, such as with the Premonstratensians, but even they Romanized their liturgy over time, often dropping sequences as part of the process. The emphasis at the time was on liturgical uniformity, particularly as the Church responded to the Reformation. Sequences written later in the Middle Ages were never seen as essential enough to warrant universal inclusion. See Gregory DiPippo, "What Really Happened to the Sequences?," *New Liturgical Movement*, May 5, 2022.

text. The document warns that such persons "will incur the wrath
of Almighty God and of the Blessed Apostles Peter and Paul." A
cursory reading might suggest that no alteration — not even the
smallest detail — could ever be permitted. Yet history reveals a
more nuanced reality. Only one year after its promulgation, Pius
V himself expanded the missal by introducing *De Defectibus* (1571),
a practical guide for clerics addressing mishaps during Mass.
Did this act provoke the divine wrath foretold in the decree?
Certainly not. While additions like this undeniably introduced
changes — altering, for instance, the rubrics or prayers available
for use — they did so not to upend the Mass but to clarify its
practice and enrich its understanding. The key distinction lies
in the nature of the change: *Quo Primum* condemned alterations
that distorted or abandoned the rite's essence, not those that
preserved its integrity while refining its execution. Subsequent
popes followed this precedent, augmenting the missal with new
feasts, prayers, and rubrics, yet always maintaining continuity
with its core tradition. Herein lies the model of authentic reform:
not novelty for its own sake, but restoration in the face of abuse
or the careful illumination of what time or neglect had obscured.

   That *Quo Primum* was received and understood as a decree that
is binding in perpetuity is shown by the actions of the successors
of Pius V. Traditionally, when a text is updated, the decree from
a predecessor at the beginning of the text is removed, and a new
decree is put in its place. This happens with all documents within
the Church regarding judicial and canonical acts.[5] However, the
Roman Missal is the only place in which this does not occur. In
a Latin Mass altar missal, one will find directly after *Quo Primum*
the document *Cum Sanctissimum* (1604) of Clement VIII. Critics
may argue that retaining Pius V's decree was merely a symbolic
nod to tradition. Yet Clement VIII's own words in *Cum Sanctissimum* clarify his intent: he explicitly states that his revisions were
made "following the example of Our Predecessors" (especially
Pius V) and "to restore the missal to its former standard" — language that mirrors Pius V's binding language in *Quo Primum*. If
Clement VIII felt bound by this document, not daring to remove
it, then so should we. Clement VIII made some minor tweaks to

---

[5] This can be seen looking through the Code of Canon Law, the Roman
Ritual, and the breviary: one will find only the issuing pope or bishop's
document and not any from a predecessor.

the missal. These included the introduction of the festal rank of *Duplex Majus* (Major Double) and the common of non-virgins. Thus, Clement VIII augmented the ranking of the saints.

Urban VIII's *Si Quid Est* (1634) reinforces this same principle. He writes that his reforms were undertaken "so that nothing may be wanting" to Pius V's original work, framing his changes as corrections to uphold—not override—the Tridentine rite's integrity. Further, he had issued this decree due to the abuse of some in the Church who were using unauthorized epistles and gospels during Mass. This shows that Clement VIII was executing authentic reform in the Roman rite. These popes' deliberate invocation of Pius V's authority in their own decrees—not merely letting his text retain its pride of place, but explicitly grounding their reforms in his mandate—suggests they viewed *Quo Primum* as binding. None of these successors revoked *Quo Primum*; instead, they positioned their revisions as fulfilling its mandate, further entrenching its perpetuity.

The final document in classical missals of the Roman rite is *Divino Afflatu* (1911) by Pope St. Pius X. Although the reforms of Pius X took place over a century ago, there is still debate as to whether his reforms were, overall, beneficial to the Church. Of the many reforms he imposed, we will highlight only his major reform to the Mass. Before Pius X's reform, many men and women had been canonized and were found worthy of commemoration at the altar. However, since antiquity, Sundays were given the rank of *Semiduplex*, which is not remarkably high on the ranking of feasts. This meant that the celebration of these saints would outrank a Sunday. A layman could go through the whole cycle of "Time after Pentecost" and never see a green chasuble at a Sunday Mass! Going to church on a Sunday, he would hear the Mass of a saint with a commemoration of the Sunday. This detracted from the purpose of the temporal cycle of the Church and deprived the faithful of some of the finest and most ancient content in the missal. Seeing this issue in the calendar, Pius X reformed the liturgy with *Divino Afflatu*, changing Sunday's ranking to the equivalent of a *Duplex* of the II Class. Precedence would thus be given to the Sunday unless there were a saint of an extremely high rank on the same day. However, Pius X did not dare to change what was written in the missal. In any *Missale Romanum* published after the reform of Pius X, you will see that the "green Sundays" still have the rank of *Semiduplex* written next to them on the page; however, they are to be treated as a *Duplex* II Class in reality. Can one say that Pius X's reform was authentic? Yes. This is evident insofar as its intention was to combat a certain unfortunate neglect of traditional content. Pius X did not impose these reforms because he believed that it would have been "nice" to see something new. These reforms were meant solely to restore to Sundays the proper dignity that they had in the past. In this sense, Pius X's reform falls under the category of clarification. However, Pius X still felt bound by his predecessors, as he added his decree after theirs and did not even change the name of Sunday's rank. This is why one can say that no new edition of the Roman Missal with notable changes came out until that of 1920, which reflected Pius X's revisions.[6]

Also worth noting is Pius X's most magnificent document, *Tra le Sollecitudini* (1903).[7] This document about the liturgy discussed a shift in priorities. Throughout the history of the Church, numerous composers have written beautiful pieces for the Mass. Polyphonic Masses were seen almost as a "norm" for Solemn Mass at certain times. There is no doubt that these beautiful motets and settings have directed the souls of many to the beauty of God. However, the original music of the Church, Gregorian chant, was suffering neglect. Recordings and other evidence from the past century indicate places of worship (cathedrals, parishes, and even seminaries) where all the focus fell on polyphonic pieces, with the Propers of the Mass chanted in psalm tone. Pius X attempted to dismantle this abuse by his document *Tra le Sollecitudini*. He insisted that "special efforts are to be made to restore the use of the Gregorian chant by the people, so that the faithful may again take a more active part in the ecclesiastical offices, as was the case in ancient times."[8] In this way, Pius X sought to restore the chant to its proper role in the liturgy. Seeing that something genuine had been lost due to abuse, he published this document to instruct, indeed to oblige, those in charge of the liturgy at all levels to restore the authentic music of the Church.

---

[6] Jungmann, *Mass of the Roman Rite*, 1:140.
[7] For a detailed commentary on this document, see Patrick John Brill, *The Great Sacred Music Reform of Pope St. Pius X* (Os Justi Press, 2024).
[8] *Tra le Sollecitudini* 3.

In the last few decades, the liturgy has been subjected to wave after wave of change in the name of so-called "reform." We need to know how to distinguish between authentic and false reform. When we look upon the changes from the sixteenth century until the turn of the twentieth century, one can see that the popes gave great thought and consideration to protecting and restoring the liturgy. They acknowledged that the liturgy is not given to man to change but rather given that man may change. Whenever something obscures or obstructs the way for man to truly participate in the liturgy, then reform is necessary. Because "the Tridentine rite reached a state of perfection, a beauty of form and fullness of content that allowed for no further substantial improvement,"[9] reform is conducted only to clarify a confusing matter or to stop unfortunate abuse. The Church should always be strict in monitoring the liturgy to ensure that what is passed on to us is duly venerated and that God may be glorified in all things.

---

[9] Kwasniewski, *Once and Future Roman Rite*, 341.

3

The Storm Gathers (1888–1954)

ODAY, QUESTIONS ARE FREQUENTLY asked about liturgical reform: "When did everything go wrong in the Church?" "When did the changes get out of hand?" "Which pope was the last good pope?" Only a future pope more sympathetic to tradition can truly answer these questions. What is attempted here is to give more clarity on these issues.

We have to understand that the Church is a perfect society. A perfect society is one that contains within it all that is needed for the perfection of its members, not one that is composed of perfect individuals. The perfect society is inhabited by imperfect people. Let us not forget that St. Peter, the first pope, denied Our Lord thrice. The papacy has been filled with men of significant greed and corruption. Does this mean that the Church herself is greedy and corrupt? No. The Church, our Mother on earth, is a loving Mother. She guides us with the help of the Holy Ghost to save souls. However, through the permissive will of God, bad men have risen through the ranks in the Church. When looking at the past century, one can track the dangerous changes made to the liturgy. The *Novus Ordo Missae* did not spring up overnight. There were particular circumstances and people that allowed this to occur. The purpose of this chapter is to examine the liturgical changes of the past century, tracing the decisions and influences that led to them. By understanding where the Church took a wrong turn, we can recognize the need to restore what was unjustly discarded.

LEO XIII: THE POPE OF THE WORKING MAN (1878–1903)

We should begin our assessment a little prior to the twentieth century, when Leo XIII occupied the chair of St. Peter. Leo XIII was a good and holy pope. In his papacy, he developed Catholic social teaching in a host of encyclicals that discussed a wide range of political and economic questions.[1] He encouraged a

---

[1] See Peter A. Kwasniewski, ed., *A Reader in Catholic Social Teaching from Syllabus Errorum to Deus Caritas Est* (Cluny Media, 2017), 20–151.

revival of scholastic theology, particularly by means of the study of St. Thomas Aquinas, in *Aeterni Patris* (1879), to fight against the rise of secularism and the first rumblings of modernism. He was well-known for his devotion to the Holy Rosary and the Sacred Heart and his care for the Oriental Churches. However, one can also see Leo XIII starting to make missteps with the liturgy. When celebrating Low Mass, Leo XIII allowed the faithful to join him in reciting the entirety of Our Father.[2] This was unheard of. In the authentic and uninterrupted Western practice, as witnessed by St. Augustine of Hippo and St. Gregory the Great, the celebrant chants the *Pater Noster* up until the last line, *et ne nos inducas in tentationem*, to which all present chant back *sed libera nos a malo* and the priest says *Amen*.[3] This calls to mind the need of the priest for his people. He cannot say Our Father without those present to complete it. Those present cannot say Our Father without the celebrant leading them. This ritualized reliance on each other expresses the communal aspect of the Mass far better than all present reciting the *Pater Noster* in its entirety. The closest we get in the West to the recitation of the Our Father by all present is the Mozarabic (Visigothic) rite, where Amen is said after every line that the celebrant sings of the *Pater Noster*, followed by the usual completion requiring the faithful and celebrant to chant the final two lines asynchronously.[4] This practice of Leo XIII's was not followed by the popes after him until the promulgation of Pius XII's 1955 Good Friday service, which in this respect served as a trial balloon for the 1958 document *De Musica Sacra et Sacra Liturgia*, which allowed the

---

[2] Mount St. Mary's Seminary & School of Theology, "Fr. Fitzgerald, 'the Liturgical Movement from Pope St. Pius X to Pope Francis: An Evaluation,'" YouTube, May 12, 2016, www.youtube.com/watch?v=K9dorKlt_bA.

[3] St. Augustine (354–430) preached to his people: "In the church, this prayer of our Lord, to which the faithful listen, is recited every day at the altar of God" (Sermon 68, ch. xiii, 12; PL 38:399). In an epistle to John of Syracuse, St. Gregory the Great (r. 590–604) writes: "The Lord's Prayer, among the Greeks, is said by all the people; among us, by the priest alone" (Bk. 9, Ep. 26; PL 77:964–65).

[4] This practice was condemned under Pius XII: "It is strictly forbidden for the faithful in unison or for a commentator to recite aloud with the priest the parts of the Proper, Ordinary, and canon of the Mass" (Sacred Congregation for Rites, *De Musica Sacra et Sacra Liturgia* — Instruction on Sacred Music and Sacred Liturgy, *Adoremus*, September 3, 1958, https://adoremus.org/1958/09/instruction-on-sacred-music/, 14).

faithful to recite the *Pater Noster* in its entirety with the priest during a Low Mass (no. 32). This, in turn, furnished the template for the *Novus Ordo*.

The liturgy-related feature for which Leo XIII is best known is the "Leonine Prayers." These prayers were to be prayed after Low Mass (except in certain circumstances) for the liberation of Papal States from the anticlerical forces of the Risorgimento. However, a later pope changed the intention to be for the liberation of Russia, reflecting Our Lady's request at Fatima.[5] These prayers were said by the celebrant and faithful after Mass. In theory, this was quite reasonable. What could ever be wrong with more prayer? However, this was the first time we have the priest still vested in the vestments exclusively worn for Mass, praying in the vernacular. The maniple and chasuble—vestments to be worn exclusively for Mass—were worn during these prayers. As a result, these prayers marked a departure from tradition regarding the understanding of vestments. If the priest were to recite the prayers having removed the chasuble or at least the maniple (as occurs at the time of the homily), there would be no issue.[6] But here, one sees a priest vested and praying in the vernacular. Some may argue that certain other sacraments were allowed to be given in the vernacular, and this is true. However, unlike a sacrament such as confession, the Mass is the sacrifice of Calvary. There is no need for the vernacular. Since antiquity, Latin has been the reserved sacred language we use to honor God in the Mass. The title over the cross was written in Greek, Hebrew, and Latin; thus it is fitting that we have only these languages at our Masses in the Roman rite, through which the mystery of the Cross is renewed upon our altars.[7] As noted above, the Leonine Prayers are technically performed outside of Mass and so are not part of Mass; yet the praying of them in the vernacular by a priest vested for Mass may have established a precedent for what appeared to be a kind of liturgical prayer with the people in the mother tongue.

---

[5] For a full history of the prayers after Mass, see Joseph Shaw, ed., *The Case for Liturgical Restoration* (Angelico Press, 2019), 195–203.

[6] See Peter Kwasniewski, "The Homily Is Not Part of the Liturgy," *The Remnant*, January 15, 2021, https://remnantnewspaper.com/web/index.php/fetzen-fliegen/item/5234-the-homily-is-not-part-of-the-liturgy.

[7] See St. Thomas Aquinas, *In IV Sent.*, Dist. 8, exp. text.

PIUS X–PIUS XI: THE UNEXPECTED (1903–1939)

Not much ill can be said about some of the reforms of Pope St. Pius X. He lowered the age of the reception of Holy Communion to the age of reason and even encouraged the frequent reception of Holy Communion for those in a state of grace. Pius X's catechism is a marvel in and of itself and is highly recommended for all Catholics to read. Pius X was a staunch enemy of modernism, as can be seen in his encyclical *Pascendi Dominici Gregis*. What cannot be ignored, however, is his allowance of parts of the Mass in the vernacular.

Pius X was the pope who popularized the distribution of Holy Communion of the faithful within the context of Mass. This ceremony was already present in the missal,[8] but it was neglected in favor of distribution of the sacrament before or after Mass. However, Pius X encouraged the faithful in the document *Sacra Tridentina* that "at each Mass the faithful who are present should communicate, not only in spiritual desire, but sacramentally."[9] Pius X was encouraging priests to return to what the rubrics decreed rather than the custom that had grown. There was no need to add this to the *Ordo Missae*, as this had always been present in the missal. The addition of the Confiteor and absolution prior to the faithful's reception of Holy Communion underlined that this reception was separate from and, in a sense, subordinated to the priest's reception, which, unlike theirs, is essential to the offering of the Mass.

When one thinks of the introduction of the vernacular into the Mass, one immediately thinks of Pope Pius XII. However, permission for the use of the vernacular for parts of the Mass had been granted on occasion long before the papacy of Pius XII, including in 1906 by Pius X (for the Propers in the Austro-Hungarian Empire).[10] This cannot be called unprecedented due to Leo XIII's allowance of the priest vested in Mass vestments reciting the Leonine Prayers in the vernacular. Pius X's successors

---

[8] *Ritus Servandus* X, 6.
[9] Decree on Frequent and Daily Reception of Holy Communion, EWTN, December 20, 1905, www.ewtn.com/catholicism/library/decree-on-frequent--daily-reception-of-holy-communion-2174.
[10] Keith F. Pecklers, *The Living Language of Christian Worship* (Liturgical Press, 2003), 32.

did the same: Benedict XV in 1920 (Croatian,[11] Slovenian, and Czech) and Pius XI in 1929 (German, in Bavaria).[12]

This all descends from an understanding that the faithful needed the vernacular so that they may understand the Mass and actively participate more fully—an idea highly favored by the early Protestant reformers, such as Cranmer. However, there are several ways to tackle this issue without the need to touch the sacred mysteries:

1. The repetition of the Epistle and Gospel in the vernacular at the sermon.

2. A sermon that weaves in the Propers of the Mass.

3. The use of hand missals. These have been in existence since the creation of the printing press. If the faithful must know what every prayer is, a hand missal is the best way to ensure such access.[13]

4. Catechesis and education of the faithful into the meaning of the various parts of the Mass.

We have always had numerous people within the Church who were illiterate. These were laymen who would attend Mass fruitfully without any sort of need to understand the readings of the day. They did not believe they had to understand every single word in the liturgy to participate. They understood the Mass as a pious sacrament of devotion, not a literature club. The practices of these pious men and women show that there was no need to have a vernacular liturgy to create saints.

There are many reasons why the liturgy is in Latin for the Roman rite. Firstly, it is the preservation of tradition. The Latin tongue unites us with our forefathers in the Faith. It is the heritage

---

[11] This, despite the Croatians having access to the Glagolitic rite of Mass, which was the Roman rite in the sacred tongue of Old Church Slavonic. Why reject their traditions and customs for a vulgar tongue? See Pecklers, *The Living Language*, 31.

[12] Pecklers, 32.

[13] For more information, see Hand Missal History (https://handmissal history.com/). One may argue that the suggestion that hand missals are a sufficient alternative to use of the vernacular does not fully account for the complexities of the historical context and the evolving needs of the faithful. Yet is this not the point of the sermon? The local priest unfolds the meaning of the readings and ceremonies for the congregation in front of him, whose needs he knows best.

of the Western Church to have Latin as the language of the liturgy, a practice upheld for generations upon generations. Latin also served as a universal tongue for believers. No matter where one journeyed within the Church, attendance at Sunday Mass would present the familiar prayers in Latin—a shared liturgical tongue, even if not fluently understood by all. This universality fostered a profound unity, as the faithful recognized the sacred words and rhythms of the rite, steeped in centuries of common use. The Latin tongue's being a "dead language" is likewise of great benefit. Lacking native speakers, the meanings ascribed to its words remain fixed, avoiding the shifts inherent to living languages. Moreover, Latin itself is sacred. It is a language Our Lord certainly knew, one inscribed on the cross and enshrined in the early writings of the Church.[14]

Even in the East, the vernacular is traditionally discouraged. Butler writes that

> all the Oriental Schismatics, how different soever, as Greeks, Ethiopians, Indians, Muscovites, etc., say Mass, but no one in the vulgar language. The Greeks use the Liturgies, which (according to their tradition) were made use of by St. Chrysostom and St. Basil; that is, in the old Greek, of which the common people understand little or nothing. This is also reluctantly acknowledged by Moshiem, who owns that the language of the Divine Service is absolutely unintelligible to the multitude. The Ethiopians and Armenians say Mass in the old Ethiopian and Armenian tongues, which none but the learned understand. The Syrians, Indians, and Egyptians say Mass in Syriac, though Arabic be their vulgar language; as it is to the Melchites and Georgians, who yet say Mass in Greek . . .[15]

Latin embodies and transmits the ancient and universal faith of the Western Church, ensuring a sacred expression of sacred content. Also, it preserves the integrity of the Mass. Vernacular translations of the scriptures are encouraged for the edification of the faithful. However, the Vulgate (translated by St. Jerome)

---

[14] For an extended treatment of Latin as the proper liturgical language of the West, see Peter Kwasniewski, *Turned Around: Replying to Common Objections Against the Traditional Latin Mass* (TAN Books, 2024), 167–190.
[15] Thomas Butler, *The Truths of the Catholic Religion* (C. Dolman, 1841), 277. See also Kwasniewski, *Once and Future Roman Rite*, 282–83.

remains the definitive and official translation of the scriptures by the Church. Although the Church has approved other translations, these are usually quite horrible in their wording and phrasing, as one can see in such versions as the Jerusalem Bible and the New American Bible. There is no reason, especially in the modern world, to have parts of the liturgy in the vernacular. With the age of the internet and the ability to print for a decent price, all have access to translations of the liturgy that do not affect the Mass itself. Thankfully, "the Church, inspired by the Holy Ghost, was aware of the baneful consequences of exposing its service to the constant changes of arbitrary and fleeting sounds; hence it determined for the preservation of the public Liturgies, to have them performed in languages like the Greek and Latin, not subject to the fluctuations experienced by the living ones."[16]

PIUS XII: THE GREAT "CONSERVATIVE" (1939–1958)

Many hold Pius XII to be the "great conservative pope of our age." However, this does not paint the most authentic image of Pius XII. Pacelli was certainly doctrinally sound; however, when it came to the liturgy, one can see he was most certainly a liberal. In many places that offer the traditional rites of the Church, it is almost considered heresy to speak ill of Pius XII. He is seen as the pope of 1950s conservatism and, therefore, the last good pope. Although Pius XII did many beneficial things for the Church, his liturgical liberalism must not be ignored.

After the election of Cardinal Pacelli to the throne of St. Peter, one of his first actions as the new pope was quite anti-traditionalist. According to a longstanding tradition, the coronation of the popes occurred within St. Peter's Basilica as an honorary tribute to the pope who first received the keys from Our Lord. However, Pius XII, in his misunderstanding of liturgical and devotional principles, changed this beautiful and historical rite. Instead of being crowned in the presence of St. Peter and the buried popes, Pius XII changed the ritual to have himself crowned on the balcony of St. Peter's. Thus, he was to be crowned in the presence of the faithful and not, symbolically, in that of St. Peter. It is worth noting that an exception to this rule was the coronation of Pope Leo XIII, who was crowned in the Sistine Chapel due to political

---

[16] Butler, *Truths of the Catholic Religion*, 277.

issues regarding the territory of the Vatican and Italian states.[17] Pius XII's decision to prioritize public visibility over tradition in his coronation best exemplifies his broader approach to the liturgy thereafter (and, incidentally, set a notable precedent for seemingly unending changes to papal ceremonies).

Pius XII, in his great "conservatism," decided to further pursue the vernacularization of the liturgy. Under his reign, the Sacred Congregation of Rites granted permission for the use of the vernacular for various parts of the Church's rites. In countries where Catholic mission activities were expanding, including Indonesia and Japan, in 1941–1942,[18] the use of a purely vernacular *Rituale* was encouraged. In 1949, permission was granted to use Mandarin (Chinese) for the entirety of Mass, except the Canon, and the same was permitted for Hindi in India in 1950. Permission was also granted for French (1948) and German (1951) translations to be used in rituals other than the Mass.[19] While insisting on the primacy of Latin in the Eucharistic liturgy of the Western Church, Pius XII here approves vernacular use in the ritual for sacraments and other rites outside the Mass. All such permissions, however, were to be granted by the Holy See.

Pius XII also saw fit to introduce the role of a "commentator" on the mysteries of the Mass. Pius XII argued that "the active participation of the faithful can be more easily brought about with the help of a commentator, especially in holy Mass, and in some of the more complex liturgical ceremonies."[20] Only the Good Lord knows why something like this would be needed at Mass. If a priest were to properly catechize his flock, there would be no need for an ongoing commentary on the Mass as though it were some sort of sports event. One may think that such a concept could be accepted in light of tradition, if it involved a cleric explaining things from the pulpit while the sacred ceremonies unfolded; however, this role could be assumed by a layman if no cleric were available![21]

---

[17] "The Coronation of Pope Leo XIII," *The Catholic World* 27, no. 158 (1878): 280–81, https://name.umdl.umich.edu/bac8387.0027.158.

[18] Pecklers, *The Living Language*, 33.

[19] Pecklers, 33.

[20] *De Musica Sacra* 96.

[21] "The role of commentator should properly be carried out by a priest or at least a cleric. If none is available, a layman of good Christian character and well instructed in his duties may fill the role" (*De Musica Sacra* 96).

Furthermore, Pius XII allowed for the use of vernacular hymns during the celebration of Mass. There has been evidence of the use of vernacular before and after Mass, but the introduction of vernacular hymns during the Mass is nothing other than a departure from tradition. At a Solemn or Sung Mass, the vernacular hymns were to follow the Latin chants.[22] However, at a Low Mass, these could occur at any time.[23] Instead of prioritizing the rich history of chant and Latin hymns written by those within the Church, vernacular hymns were introduced—some of which were written by Protestants but were seen as not being contrary to the Faith.

Pius XII added many new feasts to the calendar and even dogmatized the Assumption of Our Lady.[24] There is much debate as to the necessity of creating a new Mass for the Assumption. Even if there is nothing doctrinally wrong with the Propers, does freedom from error excuse the change in usage from the more ancient Propers? He also changed the feast day of St. Joseph, which had been observed on the third Wednesday after Easter since 1911. The feast of the patron of the universal Church has been changed several times in the past, so, in theory, there is nothing wrong with moving it again. However, the feast of St. Joseph was moved to May 1, the Communist's labor day. Was Pius XII encouraging socialism? Not at all. This was his way of trying to combat communism under the patronage of St. Joseph. It was an awkward way to go about doing it, because it meant Pius XII displaced the feasts of two apostles, Philip and James, who had been celebrated in the Roman tradition on that date going back to the foundation of the feast. Additionally, the new feast's Office is justly criticized for being a glorification of work, not so much of St. Joseph. Even today in Italy, some people jokingly describe St. Joseph's feast on May 1st as "La Festa di San Guiseppe, Il Communista."

---

[22] It is true that Pius XII made this allowance only where a "centenary of immemorial custom has obtained," such as the German-speaking countries (*Musicæ sacræ disciplina*, AAS 48 [1956]: 16–17). Nevertheless, with such toleration came growth in the number of experiments in vernacular hymnody, and it stretches credulity to say that this eventuality had not been anticipated.

[23] *De Musica Sacra* 14b.

[24] Whether this dogmatic definition was needed is debatable. Catholics had never questioned that Our Lady had been assumed into heaven.

Another example of Pius XII's liturgical modernism is his assistance in the creation and promulgation of the "Bea psalter" by the Pontifical Biblical Institute. This psalter was named after Cardinal Augustin Bea, who was the head of the project. According to Pius XII, Jerome stated that there must have been flaws in his translation of a translation (as he made use of the Septuagint), and that is why Pius XII argued for the need to translate the psalms directly from Hebrew. The project of directly translating the psalms from Hebrew started at the beginning of World War II and was released for optional use in 1945. However, it was later abandoned. The reasons why it was abandoned can be seen in the side-by-side comparison of Psalm 50 according to the Vulgate and Bea texts. Its flaws become even more apparent when it is sung for the Propers of some of the newly created feasts of Pius XII. The Bea version is awkward and stilted.

PSALM 50 IN LATIN[25]

Vulgate Psalter	Bea Psalter
50:1 Miserére mei, Deus, * secúndum magnam misericórdiam tuam.	50:1 Miserére mei, Deus, * secúndum misericórdiam tuam;
50:2 Et secúndum multitúdinem miseratiónum tuárum, * dele iniquitátem meam.	50:2 Secúndum multitúdinem miseratiónum tuárum * dele iniquitátem meam.
50:3 Ámplius lava me ab iniquitáte mea: * et a peccáto meo munda me.	50:3 Pénitus lava me a culpa mea, * et a peccáto meo munda me.
50:4 Quóniam iniquitátem meam ego cognósco: * et peccátum meum contra me est semper.	50:4 Nam iniquitátem meam ego agnósco, * et peccátum meum coram me est semper.
50:5 Tibi soli peccávi, et malum coram te feci: * ut justificéris in sermónibus tuis, et vincas cum judicáris.	50:5 Tibi soli peccávi et, quod malum est coram te, feci, * ut manifestéris iustus in senténtia tua, rectus in iudício tuo.
50:6 Ecce enim, in iniquitátibus concéptus sum: * et in peccátis concépit me mater mea.	50:6 Ecce, in culpa natus sum, * et in peccáto concépit me mater mea.

---

[25] Cantors note that chanting the Bea psalter is quite nauseating. It is often lamented that the Propers of Masses created under the reign of Pius XII use the Bea psalter. Some examples include the new Assumption Mass and the feast of Pope St. Pius X. When a person accustomed to the Vulgate reads the antiphons, it is like hitting massive speed bumps.

50:7 Ecce enim, veritátem dilexísti: * incérta et occúlta sapiéntiæ tuæ manifestásti mihi.

50:8 Aspérges me hyssópo, et mundábor: * lavábis me, et super nivem dealbábor.

50:9 Audítui meo dabis gáudium et lætítiam: * et exsultábunt ossa humiliáta.

50:10 Avérte fáciem tuam a peccátis meis: * et omnes iniquitátes meas dele.

50:11 Cor mundum crea in me, Deus: * et spíritum rectum ínnova in viscéribus meis.

50:12 Ne proícias me a fácie tua: * et spíritum sanctum tuum ne áuferas a me.

50:13 Redde mihi lætítiam salutáris tui: * et spíritu principáli confírma me.

50:14 Docébo iníquos vias tuas: * et ímpii ad te converténtur.

50:15 Líbera me de sanguínibus, Deus, Deus salútis meæ: * et exsultábit lingua mea justítiam tuam.

50:16 Dómine, lábia mea apéries: * et os meum annuntiábit laudem tuam.

50:17 Quóniam si voluísses sacrifícium, dedíssem útique: * holocáustis non delectáberis.

50:18 Sacrifícium Deo spíritus contribulátus: * cor contrítum, et humiliátum, Deus, non despícies.

50:19 Benígne fac, Dómine, in bona voluntáte tua Sion: * ut ædificéntur muri Jerúsalem.

50:20 Tunc acceptábis sacrificium justítiæ, oblatiónes, et holocáusta: * tunc impónent super altáre tuum vítulos.

50:7 Ecce, sinceritáte cordis delectáris, * et in præcórdiis sapiéntiam me doces.

50:8 Aspérge me hyssópo, et mundábor; * lava me, et super nivem dealbábor.

50:9 Fac me audíre gáudium et lætítiam, * exsúltent ossa quæ contrivísti.

50:10 Avérte fáciem tuam a peccátis meis, * et omnes culpas meas dele.

50:11 Cor mundum crea mihi, Deus, * et spíritum firmum rénova in me.

50:12 Ne proiéceris me a fácie tua, * et spíritum sanctum tuum ne abstúleris a me.

50:13 Redde mihi lætítiam salútis tuæ, * et spíritu generóso confirma me.

50:14 Docébo iníquos vias tuas, * et peccatóres ad te converténtur.

50:15 Líbera me a pœna sánguinis, Deus, Deus salvátor meus: * exsúltet lingua mea de iustítia tua.

50:16 Dómine, lábia mea apéries, * et os meum annuntiábit laudem tuam.

50:17 Neque enim sacrifício delectáris; * et holocáustum, si darem, non acceptáres.

50:18 Sacrifícium meum, Deus, spíritus contrítus, * cor contrítum et humiliátum, Deus, non despícies.

50:19 Benígne fac, Dómine, pro bonitáte tua, erga Sion, * ut reædífices muros Ierúsalem.

50:20 Tunc acceptábis sacrifícia legítima, oblatiónes et holocáusta, * tunc ófferent super altáre tuum vítulos.

The only thing left to say is *Bea culpa, Bea culpa, Bea maxima culpa!*

THE 1948 LITURGICAL COMMISSION

The Commission for Liturgical Reform was established by Pope Pius XII in Rome on May 28, 1948, and overseen by the Congregation of Rites. This Commission marked the beginning of deliberate efforts to adapt the liturgy of the Catholic Church to the modern world. This is a peculiar idea. The idea of adapting the Mass to a world entrapped in modernism was quite foolish. This Commission was the beginning of the end of the authentic Roman rite. The Commission was led by Fr. (later Cardinal) Ferdinando Antonelli, OFM; its secretary was Fr. (later Archbishop and alleged Freemason) Annibale Bugnini, CM. These men were also among the architects of the *Novus Ordo Missae*. As Bugnini stated, the Commission revolved around "ranking feasts on theological grounds," which, "although complicated, artificial and practically impossible to implement," laid the groundwork for the reform.[26] A significant step was the third supplement, which considered "historical, hagiographical and liturgical material" in order to conceptualize a calendar that later influenced the Pauline rite of 1969.[27]

Bugnini notes how the Commission's efforts marked the first step in a movement that saw the supposed restoration of the ancient Easter Vigil, accomplished in 1951, "which elicited an explosion of joy throughout the Church."[28] However, Bugnini stated that the work of the group was no longer about preserving tradition. Rather, it was about the "liturgy [being] at last launched decisively on a pastoral course,"[29] which culminated in the destruction of the ancient Holy Week rites and in the

---

[26] Annibale Bugnini, *The Reform of the Liturgy, 1948–1975* (Liturgical Press, 1990), 8, 10.

[27] See Bugnini, 8.

[28] Bugnini, 10. Alcuin Reid presents evidence to the contrary in "Holy Week Reforms Revisited — Some New Material and Paths for Further Study," in idem, ed., *Liturgy in the Twenty-First Century: Contemporary Issues and Perspectives* (Bloomsbury T&T Clark, 2016), 234–59.

[29] Bugnini, 10. To give the full quotation: "The first fruit of the commission's work was the restoration of the Easter Vigil (1951), which elicited an explosion of joy throughout the Church. It was a signal that the liturgy was at last launched decisively on a pastoral course. The same reforming principles were applied in 1955 to the whole of Holy Week and in 1960, with the Code of Rubrics, to the remainder of the liturgy, especially the Divine Office. Two years later the new typical editions of the Breviary and the Roman Pontifical were published."

new code of rubrics established in 1960. The aim of the group was to outline the steps needed to bring to birth a new liturgy in the Church, one that was adapted to the times. The Commission was officially disbanded in 1959, with the establishment of the Conciliar Preparatory Commission for the reform of the liturgy. This reveals a connection between the 1948–1959 reforms and the establishment of the *Novus Ordo Missae*. Reflecting upon the Pian Commission, Bugnini stated that when "the Council was announced and new reforming currents of thought exerted their superior pressure, the Johannine liturgical renewal lost a good deal of energy."[30] This energy would later be recovered and concentrated on the reforms that emerged from 1964–1974.

Worth mentioning as well are the liturgical conferences that took place at Maria Laach (1951), Mont Sainte Odile (1952), Lugano (1953), Mont César (1954), and Assisi (1956). It can be said that most of the reforms that took place in the 1960s had their roots in the deliberations at those conferences. The process of liturgical reform began in earnest at the Maria Laach conference in 1951, where Josef Jungmann presented a significant paper addressing the challenges of the Mass. Participants expressed considerable admiration for Pope Pius XII's recent adjustments to the Holy Saturday liturgy (which are discussed in the next chapter), though these were relatively modest compared to the reforms of 1955. Discussions at the conference focused on extending similar revisions to the Maundy Thursday and Good Friday liturgies. Jungmann proposed a "penitential rite" aimed at pastoral efficiency, and various changes, such as eliminating silence during the Eucharistic Prayer, the prayers at the foot of the altar, and the Last Gospel, were suggested. At the Mont Sainte Odile conference the following year, the theme of "Liturgy and the Modern World" was discussed. Proposals emerged for reforms later enacted, including simplifying the rubrics for the Canon of the Mass, introducing a sung doxology for the minor elevation at High Mass and an audible one at Low Mass, and abolishing the Confiteor and absolution before Communion. A simpler formula for distributing Holy Communion (just the phrase *Corpus Christi)* was also considered. In 1953, at Lugano, the concept of active participation became a focal point, with discussions about vernacular readings and

---

[30] Bugnini, 10.

a new lectionary. Notably, Cardinal Ottaviani, a key figure in later debates, was present and even celebrated Mass facing the congregation. The future Pope Paul VI, then Archbishop Montini, was also in attendance. These discussions made it clear that many of the later reforms initiated by the Consilium were being planned well in advance under the direction of Pius XII, whose leadership remained active and deliberate.[31]

It is important to note that although the Commission "worked in absolute secrecy," its members "enjoyed the full confidence of the pope."[32] This ensured that Pius XII was kept informed on their intentions and plans. Bugnini was asked to join the Commission as its secretary; he was at the time the director of a publication that spoke of supposed errors in the liturgy and the ways in which these could be mitigated.[33] The Commission enjoyed its secrecy and papal approval to the extent that its "publication of the *Ordo Sabbati Sancti instaurati* at the beginning of March 1951 caught even the officials of the Congregation of Rites by surprise."[34] Although the reforms were created by a group of individuals, they had to be signed into force by Pope Pius XII. This, in effect, implicates Pius XII for the reforms. Being the Vicar of Christ upon earth, it was his personal responsibility to safeguard the doctrine and liturgy of the Church. In Assisi, Pius XII claimed that the reforms started by the Commission were "a sign of the providential dispositions of God for the present time [and] of the movement of the Holy Spirit in the Church."[35]

---

[31] The name of Montini shows up frequently; he was both a close (though not always trusted) collaborator of Pius XII's and the one who hand-picked Bugnini to lead the postconciliar liturgical reform. As Paul VI, Montini penned these telling words in the Apostolic Constitution *Missale Romanum* (April 3, 1969) by which he published the *Novus Ordo Missae*: "There has grown and spread among the Christian people the liturgical renewal which, according to Pius XII, Our predecessor of venerable memory, seems to show the signs of God's providence in the present time, a salvific action of the Holy Spirit in His Church. This renewal has also shown clearly that the formulas of the Roman Missal ought to be revised and enriched. The beginning of this renewal was the work of Our predecessor, this same Pius XII, in the restoration of the Paschal Vigil and of the Holy Week Rite, which formed the first stage of updating the Roman Missal for the present-day mentality."

[32] Bugnini, 9.

[33] This was called *Ephemerides Liturgicae*.

[34] Bugnini, 9.

[35] International Congress Pastoral Library, *The Assisi Papers: Proceedings of*

CONCLUSION

In reflecting on the trajectory of liturgical reform over the past century, it becomes evident that each papal decision has contributed to a complex and evolving tragedy. From Leo XIII's initial allowances to the more pronounced changes under Pius XII, these developments represent more than mere administrative adjustments — they signify a profound shift. As one observes the reforms, it becomes clear that they marked a move "from structure to substance: the new ceremonies were a mutation of the old ones, not merely a reorganization of content."[36] These changes, while possibly well-intentioned, inadvertently set the stage for more significant transformations. Thus, as we discern the motivations and outcomes of these reforms, let us do so with a discerning spirit and a reverent heart, striving to uphold the essence of our sacred rites amidst an ever-evolving landscape. Through such reflection and the guidance of the Holy Spirit, we may hope to preserve the timeless sanctity of our liturgical heritage and navigate the path forward with fidelity and grace.

the First International Congress of Pastoral Liturgy, Assisi-Rome, September 18–22, 1956 (Literary Licensing, 2011), 244.
[36] Kwasniewski, Once and Future Roman Rite, 334.

4

The 1955 Reforms:
A Precursor to the New Mass?

OW, WE LOOK AT THE MOST SIGNIFI-
cant reform of the liturgy in the twentieth century,
the new rites of Holy Week. This reform was quite
controversial, and we even have evidence of a later
pope disobeying it, as we will see below. In March 1955, Pius XII
released *Cum nostra hac aetate*, a decree aimed at the supposed
simplification of the rites of the liturgy. We have included below
just the changes affecting the missal and Holy Week.

CHANGES TO THE CALENDAR AND RANKING OF FEASTS

The reforms to the liturgical calendar introduced several
specific changes. The grade and ranking of Semi-doubles were
abolished, removing a longstanding classification. Sundays
during Advent, Lent, Pentecost, and other significant periods
were elevated in rank, disrupting the traditional hierarchy established by Pius V and safeguarded by Pius X. Vigils and octaves
were redefined, which affected the structure and observance
of these important liturgical times. Many of the ancient vigils,
such as those of All Hallows' Eve and even vigils for some of
the apostles, were abolished. Feasts had their rankings reclas-
sified and commemorations were adjusted, altering the way
these observances are celebrated and remembered (or not, as
the case may be).

CHANGES TO THE *MISSALE ROMANUM*

The missal saw several incomprehensible changes. The
mandatory orations designated on lower-ranking feasts were
removed. These prayers had been offered for particular reasons,
such as the defense of the Church and the intercession of all
the saints. Their removal resulted in a loss of prayers that were
crafted to reflect the themes and intentions of specific liturgical
seasons. There were also modifications to rules for the usage of
the Credo and various prefaces. The Last Gospel, which was

usually the prologue of St. John, was to be omitted during the third Mass of Christmas and Palm Sunday. The sequence *Dies Irae*, a renowned ancient hymn from the Requiem Mass, was made optional in Masses for the departed, except on All Souls' Day or when the Mass coincides with the day of death or burial with the body present (or absent for a "reasonable" cause). These changes alter the traditional practice and diminish the continuity of established liturgical customs. These reforms might have been defensible if they had addressed genuine abuses or deviations from tradition. However, they were instead justified under the vague notion of "simplicity," which led to the unjustified abolition of longstanding liturgical practices. However, if this was not enough, the 1948 Commission for the Reform of the Liturgy (with the authority of Pius XII) saw the devastation of Holy Week.

HOLY WEEK

The rites of Holy Week were among the oldest unadulterated rites of the Church. The ancient ceremonies of the *Missa Sicca* or Dry Mass and the Mass of the Presanctified are present, the latter being the last remaining of its kind in the West. However, due to "pastoral reasons," the Commission wished to change these ancient and venerable rites.

The first changes made to Holy Week were to Holy Saturday. These were approved in the year 1950. Specifically, Cardinal Liénart (an alleged Freemason[1]) "petitioned Pius XII for permission to celebrate the Easter Vigil at night rather than in the morning"[2] for pastoral reasons.[3] In response, the Cardinal was given a new

---

[1] Maquis de la Franquerie, *L'infaillibilité pontificale. Le Syllabus, la condamnation du modernisme et la crise actuelle de l'Église. Conférences*, 2nd ed. (Diffusion de la pensée française, 1974), 28.

[2] Rama Coomaraswamy, *The Destruction of the Christian Tradition* (World Wisdom, 2006), 246.

[3] It is worth noting that the changes of the times of Holy Week were and are generally accepted. Some consider this to be the only positive reform to Holy Week under the reign of Pius XII. After all, it does not seem to make much sense singing *O beata Nox* in the morning. Yet the *Missale Romanum* itself had already indicated the times when these ceremonies should take place. For instance, for Palm Sunday, the missal says that the ceremony begins once Terce has been said; Good Friday's rubrics in the missal begin with *in choro dicta nona*; the Paschal Vigil itself begins with the rubric *dicat nona in choro*. The traditional times for canonical hours are

rite with optional prayers, the use of the vernacular, and directions for the celebrant to sit and listen to the Lessons.[4] This can
be seen as a precursor to what was to be achieved in 1955.

Now we move on to the detestable changes of 1955.

PALM SUNDAY

Most of the changes for Palm Sunday concerned the ceremonies that precede the Mass. One of the major differences is
the removal of the *Missa Sicca* (Dry Mass). This was a relic of a
Mass that included the blessing of the palms.[5] Traditionally, an
important blessing was not done simply with an *Oremus* and a
few signs of the cross. An important blessing was done with a
consecratory preface. This means that it started with *Dominus
vobiscum. Et cum spiritu tuo. Sursum corda* and so on. This is seen

---

given in their names—Terce, being the third hour (9:00 a.m.), Sext the
sixth (noon), and None the ninth (3:00 p.m.). We can see from this that
Pius XII's reform meant to restore what was proper to the celebration of
the ceremonies. Over time, due to the fasting requirements, these canonical hours were anticipated, that is, said before the appointed times. Pius
XII, wishing to rectify this, restored most of the Holy Week ceremonies
to their supposed correct times. However, there is much debate on this
issue. Gregory DiPippo has written: "Ironically, the best known of these
partial restorations is the most partial, the timing of the Triduum ceremonies. It is an authentic and ancient custom to celebrate the Mass
of the Lord's Supper in the evening, and one to which no reasonable
person should object. But the celebration of the Easter vigil during the
night, the supposed greatest triumph and restoration of 1955, and the
earliest (permitted *ad experimentum* in 1951), is completely inauthentic,
and, like most of the innovations of 1955, based on an historical false-
hood" ("Bad Scholarship on the Easter Vigil," *New Liturgical Movement*,
May 14, 2020, www.newliturgicalmovement.org/2020/05/bad-scholarship-
on-easter-vigil.html).

[4] Coomaraswamy, *Destruction of the Christian Tradition*, 246.

[5] According to Fr. Aaron Williams: "In the pre-1955 Palm Sunday liturgy, the
rite for the blessing and distribution of Palms constitutes nearly an entirely
separate Mass (or a so-called 'Dry Mass of the Palms'). The reason for this
was that formerly when the Pope celebrated this rite in Rome, two Masses
were offered—one at St. Lawrence Outside-the-Walls and a second at St.
John Lateran, with a procession with palms taking place between the two.
Eventually, the location of this Mass was moved to St. Peter's and the canons
of the basilica gathered with the Pope beforehand at the oratory of St. Maria
in Turri for the blessing of palms" ("Holy Weeks Past and Present," https://
adoremus.org/2021/03/holy-weeks-past-and-present/). It should be noted
that some writers (e.g., Cardinal Schuster, Philip Goddard in *Festa Paschalia*)
do not think there was a full Mass associated with the blessing of palms.

28   LUMEN CHRISTI

most evidently in the Sacrifice of the Mass with the consecration
of the Host, beginning with the Preface before the *Canon Missae*. It is also seen in the old consecration of the paschal candle
according to the pre-1955 rites and in various ceremonies, such
as the ordination of a priest or consecration of a bishop.[6] The
consecratory ceremonies and preface for the blessing of palms
were removed by Pius XII, and all that remains is a simple
Oremus with only one of the several prayers for the blessing
of palms.[7]

Another oddity was that the color of the procession changed
from violet to red. Processions were traditionally seen as penitential, hence most processions are celebrated in violet. For
Palm Sunday, this is because it was the day when Jesus processed
to Jerusalem, where He would be slain on the cross. It is a time
of mourning, hence the use of violet. Also in the procession
was seen the use of the folded chasuble by the deacon and
subdeacon. This is another aspect of the mournful nature of
the procession. The use of red for the blessing and procession
makes no sense, as red had been liturgically reserved for days
on which martyrs have died, as well as Pentecost. Why would
red be used when Jesus had not yet been martyred? Also used
in the post-1955 Palm Sunday are the tunicle and dalmatic, the
two vestments of joy.[8] Palm Sunday was not a day of immense
joy, but rather the beginning of the great sorrowful sacrifice of
God on the cross. For this, such symbolism of joy seems quite
inappropriate.

Below follows a comparison of ceremonies between the traditional Holy Week and the Pacellian Holy Week.

---

[6] Further, it is seen in the missal of 1962 with the blessing of Easter water.
[7] Worth noting is the fact that one of the prayers removed asked that the
palms assist in the dispelling of evil wherever they are kept.
[8] That they are vestments of joy can be seen in the prayers said by the deacon
and the subdeacon when putting on the dalmatic and tunicle respectively:
"Clothe me, O Lord, with the garment of salvation and the vestment of
joy, and ever encompass me with the dalmatic of justice" and "May the
Lord clothe me in the tunicle of delight and the garment of rejoicing." See
Kwasniewski, *Once and Future Roman Rite*, 356–57.

Missa Sicca and Procession	*Blessing and Procession*
1. The celebrant is dressed in a violet stole and cope. The deacon and subdeacon are dressed in folded chasubles. The deacon wears his stole underneath and vests in the broad stole, eventually.	1. The celebrant is dressed in a red stole and cope. The deacon and subdeacon are dressed in the dalmatic and tunicle. The deacon wears his stole underneath.
2. *Missa Sicca* (Dry Mass) for the blessing of palms. This contains an Epistle, Gradual, Gospel, Preface, and Sanctus. This is done with the sacred ministers lined up in front of the missal on the Epistle side with the palms blessed on the epistle side of the altar. After the (dry) Sanctus, the priest consecrates the palms, which are located near the altar.	2. The *Missa Sicca* has been suppressed, with the Epistle, Gradual, Preface, and Sanctus removed. Blessing of palms takes place on a table, facing the people, and need not be in a church.
3. Many prayers for the blessing of palms, one of which is the consecratory preface.	3. Most of the traditional prayers for the blessing of palms were suppressed.
4. Violet for procession. The cross remained veiled in purple for the procession.	4. Red is used for the procession. The cross may be unveiled for the procession.
5. When the procession has returned to the door, two cantors go to the locked doors of the church and sing the *Gloria Laus*, which is repeated by the people.	5. The doors to the church remain open the entire time, and the *Gloria Laus* is one of many options for the chant.
6. The subdeacon strikes the door thrice with the foot of the cross, signifying the request for entrance into the heavenly Jerusalem.	6. There is no striking of the door by the subdeacon; everyone simply enters the church.
7. The *Ingrediente Domino* is sung as the cross passes through the door.	7. The *Ingrediente Domino* starts when the celebrant passes through the door.
8. The procession ends, and Mass begins as usual, with the prayers at the foot of the altar.	8. The procession ends with a prayer that was recently composed and is said facing the people.
Mass	*Mass*
1. The Passion is distinct from the Gospel of the Mass.	1. The Passion is the Gospel of the Mass.
2. The Passion begins with the institution of the Eucharist.	2. The Passion begins after the institution of the Eucharist.[9]

---

9 See Peter Kwasniewski, "The Excision of the Institution Narratives from

HOLY MONDAY

Traditional Holy Week	Pius XII's Holy Week
The seasonal prayers "against the Church's persecutors" and "for the pope" are said.	These prayers were suppressed.

HOLY TUESDAY AND SPY WEDNESDAY

Traditional Holy Week	Pius XII's Holy Week
The Passion begins with the institution of the Eucharist.	The Passion begins after the institution of the Eucharist.

MAUNDY THURSDAY

Relatively little was changed in the liturgy of Maundy Thursday. The biggest change in the Pacellian reforms concerned the rite of the *Mandatum* and its place after the homily at Mass. Prior to these reforms, the *Mandatum* was performed after Mass, and it was not to be at the high altar but in a side chapel, sacristy, or hall near the church.[10] All the other changes were due to the removal of the Mass of the Presanctified on Good Friday. Also worth noting is that the traditional Holy Week asks for a "place of repose" that should be distinct from an altar. This is a temporary setup used only for this purpose. It is thought to draw a connection to Our Lord whilst jailed.

Traditional Holy Week	Pius XII's Holy Week
1. The *Mandatum* (washing of feet) is a separate ceremony that takes place outside of Mass. It is also not to be done in the sanctuary.	1. The *Mandatum* may occur right after the homily and in the sanctuary; otherwise it may be done outside of Mass.
2. A second large Host is consecrated for the Mass of the Presanctified. This is then put into a chalice and processed to the place of repose.	2. There is no consecration of a second large Host for Good Friday.
3. Communion is distributed from Hosts consecrated at any Mass.	3. Communion is distributed from Hosts consecrated at the Mass of Maundy Thursday.

Pius XII's Holy Week," *New Liturgical Movement*, July 8, 2024. The *Novus Ordo* rectifies this mistake by having the Passion begin with the institution of the Eucharist.

[10] Adrian Fortescue, *The Ceremonies of the Roman Rite Described* (Burns, Oates & Washbourne, 1920), 290.

4. The procession has two thurifers incensing the Blessed Sacrament.	4. Use of more than one thurifer was customary previously; in 1955 the use of a single thurifer is standardized.
5. At the stripping of the altars, the veiled cross and two candlesticks remain.	5. At the stripping of the altars, the cross and candlesticks are removed, thus leaving everything bare.
6. Vespers is sung directly after Mass.	6. Those who attend the liturgy are dispensed from Vespers.

GOOD FRIDAY

The changes in the liturgy of Good Friday are the most grievous of the entire Holy Week "reform" of 1955. The Pacellian reform removed the only Mass of the Presanctified left in the Latin Church. The traditional understanding of Good Friday was that it was a Mass of the "Presanctified," which means that it was a ceremony that had the character of a Mass but with a Host consecrated at a previous Mass. The ceremony retained the nature of a Mass, as seen by the use of the chasuble and maniple, the vestments that can be worn only within Mass. The ceremonies are ancient in origin, with prayers taken from the Mass itself as well as having an elevation of the Host.

The 1955 reforms turned the liturgy of Good Friday into the modern-day equivalent of a Liturgy of the Word, with the ancient prayers that called upon the sacrifice of Calvary and the actions associated with them replaced by a simple Communion service. The procession of the Blessed Sacrament that calls to mind the procession of Christ to stand before Pilate had lost some of its dignity and honor.

Traditional Holy Week	*Pius XII's Holy Week*
1. Called: "Mass of the Presanctified" or *Feria Sexta in Parasceve*, i.e., Friday of Preparation.	1. Called: "Solemn Liturgical Action" or "Commemoration of the death of Our Lord Jesus Christ."
2. The crucifix and candlesticks are on the altar.	2. The altar is entirely bare.
3. The celebrant in a black chasuble and deacon and subdeacon in folded chasubles prostrate themselves before the altar. In the meantime, a single cloth is spread upon the altar.	3. The sacred ministers, wearing only albs and stoles, prostrate themselves before the altar. The altar is dressed at a later moment.
4. The celebrant always wears a chasuble. The sacred ministers wear maniples.	4. The priest changes between black chasuble and cope. The sacred ministers eventually change into violet vestments. Maniples are omitted.

5. The Gospel is distinct from the Passion.

5. The Passion is the Gospel of the ceremony.

6. The seventh oration is entitled "for heretics and schismatics."

6. The seventh oration is entitled "for the unity of the Church."

7. No genuflection for the oration for the Jews.[11]

7. All genuflect at the oration for the Jews.

8. The crucifix is removed from the altar and laid upon a violet cushion (covered in white silk) on the bottom step of the altar and is venerated by ministers and clergy with threefold genuflections and feet unshod.

8. The crucifix is processed from the sacristy and held by two acolytes at the footpace to be venerated by the ministers and clergy.

9. All present venerate the cross in this manner: all take off their shoes; they come in pairs, making three full prostrations; the one on the right venerates before the one on the left.

9. All approach to venerate the cross. Removal of shoes is optional. Individuals (not pairs) approach, making a simple genuflection three times.

10. The procession from the place of repose is in black vestments.

10. The procession is in violet vestments.

11. The Blessed Sacrament is processed from the altar of repose to the high altar. The *Vexilla Regis* is sung at this point.

11. The procession from the altar of repose is downplayed. The *Vexilla Regis* is not sung.

12. The procession has two thurifers walking backwards, incensing the Blessed Sacrament.

12. The rubrics do not call for the use of incense. However, some commentators suggest this should be done.

13. After the Blessed Sacrament returns to the High Altar, the sacred ministers prostrate themselves in a genuflection while *in plano*.[12] From there, the Blessed Sacrament is incensed.

13. The incensation of the Host and the double genuflection are suppressed.

14. The Victim and altar are incensed in the usual manner as at Mass.

14. The incensation of the altar is suppressed.

15. Just as Jesus was raised upon the cross, the priest takes the Host and raises it with one hand for the faithful to see and venerate.

15. Elevation of the Host suppressed.

16. The *Orate Fratres* is said without a response. The prayers that follow refer to the sacrifice.

16. The *Orate Fratres* is suppressed, as are most of the prayers mentioning the sacrifice.

---

[11] The genuflection was anciently done but was removed by the Carolingians, whence the custom spread until it was universal.

[12] At the foot of the altar.

17. The majority of the *Pater Noster* is recited by the priest alone.	17. The *Pater Noster* is recited in its entirety by all present.
18. A fraction of the Host is placed into a chalice prepared with water and wine.	18. A fraction of the Host is not placed in the chalice (a chalice is not used at all).
19. Only the priest communes.	19. Holy Communion is offered to all.
20. Vespers is sung directly after the Mass of the Presanctified.	20. Those who attend the ceremony are dispensed from Vespers.

EASTER VIGIL

One of the major issues with the Vigil is the change in the manner in which the consecratory preface, that is, the *Exsultet*, is used. The very text of the *Exsultet* proclaimed by the deacon speaks of the consecration of the candle. Pius XII transferred the blessing of the candle from the *Exsultet* to a newly constructed rite at the fire; the priest blesses the candle with a newly created prayer instead of the deacon consecrating it with the consecratory preface, which renders the *Exsultet* an oddly empty observance, retained for poetry and drama but not causally related to the actions it dictates. Also, the very ancient triple candle was removed with the swipe of a pen. This was an ancient symbol of the light borne by the Holy Trinity descending upon the world. In its place, the paschal candle is used. This shows a clear departure from the traditional understanding. In the older rites, the focus is on Christ, the light of the world. However, in the newer rites, the focus is now on the candle itself. One thing that was an invention and not a restoration was the removal of the prayers at the foot of the altar before Mass—as if the mere fact that some ceremonies occurred before the beginning of the Mass means that the sacred ministers should just be able to go straight up to the altar without observing the careful, reverential pause of due preparation before ascending the mountain of the Lord!

Also worth noting is that the Vigil of Pentecost (also called Whitsun Eve) had a character similar to that of the Easter Vigil. There was the blessing of water, the procession of the paschal candle, and the chanting of Lessons. This ceremony, dating back to antiquity, was removed by the stroke of Pius XII's pen.[13]

---

[13] There was also an attempted (partial) restoration of this Vigil in the *Novus Ordo Missae.*

Traditional Holy Week	*Pius XII's Holy Week*
1. The fire is to be started with flint.	1. The fire is to be lit in any manner before the start of ceremonies.
2. The paschal candle stands unlit in the sanctuary.	2. The paschal candle is to be blessed outside the church by the priest, and the grains of incense are never blessed; they are inserted prior to the procession.
3. The fire and grains of incense are blessed outside the church. The fire is then given to a small tapper which is used to light the *tricereo*, the rod that holds three candles.	3. The candle is used to carry the flame into the sanctuary.
4. At *Lumen Christi*, all genuflect to the flame. The flame is then held in the sanctuary on the tricereo and is not passed to the paschal candle.	4. At *Lumen Christi*, all genuflect to the candle. The flame is slowly passed to the people.
5. The *Exsultet* begins with the candle unlit, and the grains of incense are inserted at certain points. At another point, the candle is lit from the *tricereo*, which was itself lit from the Easter fire.	5. The candle is placed in the sanctuary after the *Lumen Christi*. The *Exsultet* begins with the candle already lit.
6. The *Exsultet* is the deacon's consecration of the candle.	6. The candle is incensed by the deacon walking around clockwise with a thurible.
7. There are twelve Lessons.	7. Only four of the twelve Lessons remain.
8. The blessing of water takes place in the baptistery after a procession with the paschal candle. The litany is sung after the blessing of the water. The litany is doubled.	8. Water is blessed in the middle of the sanctuary, facing the people. The litany begins after the Lessons, then there is a pause for the blessing of paschal water, and then it continues. The litany is not doubled.
9. The *Pater Noster* is sung only at the usual time by the priest, with the people making the final response.	9. A newly-created renewal of baptismal promises is recited and the *Pater Noster* is said or sung by everyone.
10. Prayers at the foot of the altar are recited.	10. Prayers at the foot of the altar are omitted.
11. Mass ends with a contracted form of Vespers.	11. Mass ends with a contracted form of Lauds.

The above comparison shows what was lost when the Pacellian rites were decreed. One can see the significant loss in the history and dignity of the rites. The ancient rites that were passed down from the origins of the Holy Mother Church were modified to become more relevant to modern man. Did every cleric enjoy these reforms? No. Not even all the popes! When John XXIII ascended the throne, he refused to partake in the Pacellian Good Friday.[14] This deliberate choice to follow the older liturgy — despite the reformed *Ordo Hebdomadae Sanctae Instauratus* (1955–1956) being in force — suggests he either questioned the legitimacy of the changes or viewed them as experimental. His adherence to the traditional rite implies a degree of skepticism toward the reform's pastoral and theological coherence.[15] It is interesting to note that when the *Novus Ordo* was released, the only defects of the 1955 Holy Week to be repaired were the re-inclusion of the institution narratives in the Passions and the re-introduction of more readings for the Vigil. It seemed that those who crafted the *Novus Ordo Missae* were, overall, quite happy with these Pacellian "reforms" of Holy Week.[16] It is obvious that "the 1955 Holy Week was a signal that the liturgy was at last launched decisively on a pastoral course."[17] The deep cuts and modifications of Holy Week

---

[14] Stefano Carusi, IBP, "The Reform of Holy Week in the Years 1951–1956" *Rorate Caeli*, July 25, 2010, https://rorate-caeli.blogspot.com/2010/07/reform-of-holy-week-in-years-1951-1956.html.

[15] Carusi, "The Reform of Holy Week." Some have argued that John XXIII would never have use a pre-55 rite due to the media storm it would have occasioned, and that the photo on the following page shows only that he opted to use a pillow instead of having the crucifix held up. However, what is shown there certainly does not follow the 1955 rubrics; and since the ceremonies were done in the Sistine Chapel, with almost no photos permitted, very few people could have known about it, and no firestorm would have been provoked.

[16] This is the overwhelming impression one receives when reading the 2005 address by Fr. Carlo Braga, a close collaborator of Archbishop Bugnini's and a member of the post-conciliar Liturgical Commission, celebrating the fiftieth anniversary of Pius XII's *Maxima Redemptionis Nostrae Mysteria*. See "Fr Carlo Braga on the 1955 Holy Week Reform," *New Liturgical Movement*, June 1–4, 2022. Speaking of the principles at the foundation of the Pius XII Holy Week, he declares: "Its principles, even within their limits, continue to be valid, and we find them, completed and updated, at the basis of the current liturgical books renewed by the post-conciliar reform, and they still influence our pastoral action and our spirituality in living the mystery of Easter" (www.newliturgicalmovement.org/2022/06/fr-carlo-braga-on-1955-holy-week-reform_4.html).

[17] Bugnini, *Reform of the Liturgy*, 10.

are part of the downfall of liturgy in the twentieth century. Given what occurred, we cannot avoid asking the following question: why should Holy Week ceremonies that were in force for only approximately fourteen years (1955–1969) be more important or binding than the rites of Holy Week that the Church observed for so many centuries, even in some respects back into antiquity? Unquestionably, the pre-1955 Holy Week has the first claim on our allegiance as Catholics who love the Latin liturgical tradition of the Church.[18]

John XXIII celebrating the "abolished" pre-Pius XII Good Friday ceremonies.

---

[18] For further reading, see Carusi, "The Reform of Holy Week"; Shawn Tribe, "The Ceremonies of Good Friday in the Papal Chapel and St. Peter's as Described in 1839," *Liturgical Arts Journal*, April 15, 2022, www.liturgicalartsjournal.com/2022/04/the-ceremonies-of-good-friday-in-papal.html.

5

1958–1960 Simplicity: The Shortcut to Mediocrity

NFORTUNATELY, THE REFORMS OF Pope Pius XII did not end with the destruction of the ancient Holy Week ceremonies. One can say that Pius XII believed that there was a need for more active participation of the faithful within the liturgy. This sounds familiar, doesn't it? Later, Paul VI delivered several papal addresses on the implementation of the *Novus Ordo*, in which he demanded that the faithful participate in every word and phrase required in the Mass.[1] Did Pius XII have a role in this? According to some, yes. There are even books and articles dedicated to Pius XII as the father of the Second Vatican Council and subsequent liturgical reform.[2] Pius XII's view on the liturgy and the perceived need for simplification was followed by all the popes after him.

HOLY COMMUNION

Let us first examine the significant reforms introduced by Pope Pius XII regarding requirements for fasting before the reception of Holy Communion at Mass — reforms that, while seemingly benign, had profoundly negative repercussions for the Church's spiritual discipline.

In 1953, Pope Pius XII issued the apostolic constitution *Christus Dominus*. This reform marked a pivotal shift in the Church's fasting regulations. Before this, the faithful were required to abstain from all food and drink from midnight until the reception of Communion, a discipline that goes back to the age of the Church Fathers. However, *Christus Dominus* introduced a notable relaxation: drinking water was no longer considered breaking the fast. Additionally, *Christus Dominus* relaxed the fasting requirements

---

[1] For the texts of the three relevant audiences (November 19 and 26, 1969, with March 17, 1965 also taken into account), see Kwasniewski, *Once and Future Roman Rite*, 381–91; for commentary on their significance, see ibid., 109–43.
[2] Nicola Bux, Peter Gumpel, and Alexandra von Teuffenbach, *Pio XII e Il Concilio* (Cantagalli Publishers, 2012).

for specific groups—namely, the sick, travelers, those engaged in strenuous physical labor, and priests celebrating multiple Masses in one day for pastoral reasons. Although these adjustments were intended to ease the burdens on the faithful, they began to undermine the uniformity and tradition of the fasting practice, which took away from the dignity and holiness of the Eucharist.

The second stage of reform came in 1957 with the apostolic constitution *Sacram Communionem*. This decree replaced the midnight fast with a new rule: a three-hour fast from solid food and alcohol and a one-hour fast from other liquids. For ordinary communicants, this meant calculating their fasting period up to the moment of receiving Communion, while priests based their fast on the time that they commenced celebrating Mass. Although this reform aimed to provide greater flexibility and made it feasible to schedule evening Masses, which the midnight fast had rendered impractical, it had significant negative consequences. By facilitating evening Masses, the reform unintentionally weakened the spiritual discipline associated with fasting. The shift from a rigorous midnight fast to a more relaxed discipline diminished the sacrificial aspect of preparation for the Eucharist, thus affecting the depth of spiritual engagement and preparation. It is interesting to juxtapose Pius XII's reforms on Holy Communion with those of Pius X. Pius X kept the same discipline of fasting but lowered the minimum age of communicants and asked for frequent holy and reverent Communions. On the other hand, Pius XII simply lowered the fasting requirements, hoping that this would have the same effect. It is hard to believe that the only thing stopping the faithful from receiving Our Lord in the Blessed Sacrament was a light fast.

To summarize, while Pope Pius XII's reforms were intended to alleviate practical difficulties and increase accessibility, they ultimately diluted the spiritual rigor that had traditionally marked fasting before Communion. This shift, while pragmatic, arguably undermined the profound sacramental preparation that fasting once embodied.

THE DIALOGUE MASS

Next, we will speak of the dreaded Dialogue Mass, sadly still present in some places that offer the traditional Mass. While Pope Pius XII's endorsement of this form of participation was seen as a positive development, it is essential to scrutinize the underlying errors and drawbacks associated with it.

At its core, the Mass is a profound act of worship that inherently calls forth the participation of all present, each fulfilling a specific key role. The most crucial aspect of this participation is interior: it involves the faithful paying devout attention and lifting their hearts to God in prayer. This interior engagement enables the faithful to be intimately united with Christ the High Priest, offering the sacrifice in unity with Him, as articulated in Pope Pius XII's encyclical *Mediator Dei* (November 20, 1947). While interior participation is paramount, the participation of the congregation can be enhanced through exterior acts. These include postures such as kneeling, standing, and sitting, as well as ceremonial signs and, notably, responses, prayers, and singing. This external participation reflects the faithful's interior disposition and reinforces their engagement with the sacred mysteries of the Mass. In *Mediator Dei*, Pope Pius XII expressed support for this external form of participation, commending efforts to involve the congregation more actively in the sacred ceremonies. He advocated for the congregation to respond to the priest's words, sing hymns appropriate to various parts of the Mass, and participate in alternating liturgical chants during solemn ceremonies.[3] Worth noting is that much of this was already the custom for Solemn Masses, where the faithful sing the ordinary chants of the Mass, such as the Gloria and the Credo. What was obscure about this document was the introduction of congregational singing into the Low Mass. So passes away the quiet, reflective nature of the Low Mass.

However, despite these well-intentioned reforms, the Dialogue Mass introduced certain errors that merit scrutiny. Firstly, while external participation, such as responses and hymns, can deepen the devotion of the faithful, if not enacted properly it can overshadow the primary focus, which should be interior devotion. The emphasis on vocal and physical participation caused an inadvertent shift from a focus on deep spiritual union with Christ to outward gestures and activity in worship. This can lead worshipers to feel uncomfortable focusing on their devotions, as they feel that they must vocally participate with the rest of the gathered people or

---

[3] *Acta Apostolicae Sedis*, vol. 39 (Libreria Editrice Vaticana, 1947), 521.

else they shall be judged as not actually taking part in the Mass. This could lead to a superficial engagement with the Mass rather than a deep, contemplative participation. The danger lies in the possibility that external acts of participation might become ends in themselves rather than expressions of an interior devotion that should remain central, as if simply saying the responses of the server at Mass is to have done all that can and should be done. In this instance, there is no growing in intimacy with Christ; there is no union with the devotion and the oblation of the Mass. In a sense, it is lip service without the service of the heart.

Moreover, the expectation for the congregation to actively respond and engage in the liturgical dialogue imposes an undue burden on those who may not be familiar with or capable of such active involvement.

While Pope Pius XII's endorsement of the Dialogue Mass aimed to foster a more engaged and participatory liturgical experience, it inadvertently introduced or gave cover to certain errors. The emphasis on external participation risks overshadowing the essential interior devotion and creates a performative approach to the Mass that detracts from its true end. As we reflect on these developments, it is crucial to balance exterior engagement with the profound interior disposition that lies at the heart of the liturgical celebration.

If one combines the previous reforms of Pius XII (the use of vernacular hymns and readings, the Bea psalter, the destruction of Holy Week, and so on) with the relaxing and lessening of the Communion fast and the push for the Dialogue Mass, one may clearly see what the plan was. There was an attempt to make the faithful participate in the Mass primarily in an external mode, which was confused with actual participation. Although the intention was good, the execution was simply reckless. All these supposed "reforms" were not reforms in the authentic sense. There was no attempt to restore, only to innovate. By trying to adopt new measures to attract people to attending Mass and receiving Holy Communion, we can say that the faithful suffered. Countless saints were able to achieve profound union with God without the use of the Dialogue Mass, vernacular, or an easing of discipline. Before these reforms, the faithful were not expected to respond to everything the priest said, as this was the role of the servers or ministers. The faithful were seen as being led by the priest and represented by the servers at Mass. The distinctive hierarchy of the Church presented in the liturgy would slowly become more blurred from this point onwards.[4]

There was much potential for authentic reform that sadly did not materialize. What might this have looked like? Simply look at the influential figures of the Liturgical Movement of the nineteenth century, such as Dom Prosper Guéranger.

While the Church is looking for better methods and engagement, God is looking for holier men. That is all that He is looking for. The Church should be aiming to raise men to holiness, but lip service and vulgar tongues in the liturgy are not how one does this. The Church gains nothing, not even souls, by lowering the bar.

From Gerald Ellard's *Mass of the Future*, published in 1948.[5]

---

[4] On the violence done to the venerable tradition of differentiated ministerial hierarchy and the correlative damage of a denigration of the proper lay vocation, see Peter Kwasniewski, *Ministers of Christ: Recovering the Roles of Clergy and Laity in an Age of Confusion* (Crisis Publications, 2021).
[5] John Paul Sonnen, "The First Permanent Altar Facing the People in the United States," *Liturgical Arts Journal*, December 3, 2024, www.liturgicalartsjournal.com/2024/12/the-first-permanent-altar-facing-people.html.

6

1960–1965:
The Age of Aquarius

WHILE NOWADAYS IT IS THE MISSAL OF 1962, called the last *editio typica* before the Council, that is most often used in celebrations of the "traditional Latin Mass," this missal is quite different from its predecessors. An entirely new set of rubrics was created and published under John XXIII in the year 1960, entirely replacing the 1570 rubrics still in force until then. While these rubrics took effect in 1960, additional modifications were introduced between then and the end of 1962. The last of these was the inclusion of St. Joseph in the Canon, which will be discussed later.

Archbishop Annibale Bugnini, the architect of the *Novus Ordo Missae*, said the following of the missal of John XXIII: "It is a bridge which opens the way to a promising future."[1] Please take note that this is his comment about *the 1962 missal*, not the 1969 missal! That such a man as Bugnini would enjoy its use — this alone should raise our suspicion. The 1962 missal was shaped by the principles of the modernist pseudo-liturgical movement. Bugnini described this missal as a "compromise" — a temporary measure on the path to creating a liturgy that would be a "new city in which the man of our age can live and feel at ease." As a transitional work, this particular missal was only in use for a brief period of two to three years. The 1948 Commission's key achievements (according to Bugnini) were "the restoration of the Easter Vigil (1951)" and the 1960 code of rubrics, together with "the new typical editions of the Breviary and the Roman Pontifical."[2]

So, what were the changes to the Tridentine Mass in the 1962 missal?

---

[1] Daniel L. Dolan, "The Pius X and John XXIII Missals Compared," www.traditionalmass.org/articles/article.php?id=18. Citing this information does not imply agreement with the ecclesiology espoused by the website.
[2] Bugnini, *Reform of the Liturgy*, 10.

Category	Changes
General	New ranking of feasts established. Use of the biretta limited.[3] Bows towards the crucifix changed.
Prayers at the Foot of the Altar	Omitted on: 1. The Purification after the Procession. 2. Ash Wednesday after the distribution of ashes. 3. Palm Sunday after the Procession. 4. Holy Saturday. 5. The four Rogation Days after the Procession. 6. And certain other Masses according to the new rubrics of the 1962 Roman Pontifical.
Collects	Seasonal Collects removed. Multiple Collects discouraged.[4]
Saints	Commemoration of a lower-ranking feast of a saint or a Sunday is either abolished or strictly curtailed so that on an ordinary Sunday, most saints' feasts entirely disappear.
Lessons on Ember Days	Some lessons were made optional. A shorter Mass was provided for Ember Saturdays.
Epistle	The celebrant at Solemn Mass sits at the sedilia and listens, no longer doubling the reading.
Sequence	The *Dies Irae* at a daily Requiem High Mass is optional.
Gospel	The celebrant at Solemn Mass listens and does not recite beforehand.

---

[3] "Comparisons," Restore the 54, accessed March 4, 2025, www.restorethe54.com/comparisons/.

[4] Prior to the reforms of John XXIII, any feast below a *Duplex* ranking would have the "seasonal Collects." These are a selection of orations that vary according to the liturgical season. It was also at the discretion of the celebrant to add any commemorations he saw fit. For instance, a priest may add a commemoration for peace in times of war, or he may be assisting the faithful in a novena and add a "votive Collect" of a saint. Traditionally, the priest was allowed up to seven commemorations at a Mass. This would only be allowed on days where the rubrics permitted the practice. However, John XXIII's rubrics established new principles:

The plan for admitting commemorations is this:

a) on 1st class liturgical days and in sung non-conventual Masses, no commemoration is admitted except a privileged one;

b) on 2nd class Sundays, only one commemoration is admitted, namely of a 2nd class feast, which, however, is omitted if a privileged commemoration is to be made;

c) on other 2nd class liturgical days, only one commemoration is admitted, namely either one privileged or one ordinary commemoration;

d) on 3rd and 4th class liturgical days, only two commemorations are admitted.

Creed	Suppressed on many feasts (doctors of the Church, St. Mary Magdalene, the angels, and so on).
Canon	St. Joseph added to the Canon.
Communion of the Faithful	Confiteor and absolution before Communion of the faithful removed.
Benedicamus Domino	Abolished, except when there is a procession after Mass.
Last Gospel	The Proper Last Gospel is abolished with the exception of Palm Sunday when palms are not blessed. No Last Gospel at all is recited for: 1. The third Mass of Christmas. 2. Palm Sunday. 3. Holy Thursday. 4. Holy Saturday. 5. Any Mass followed by a procession. 6. Requiem Masses followed by the Absolution. 7. And certain other Masses according to the new rubrics of the 1962 Roman Pontifical.

For clarity, let's examine the missal before the reforms of the 1960s.

RANKING OF FEASTS AND THE CALENDAR

The traditional ranking of feasts is as follows:

Duplex I Classis (Double of the I Class)
Duplex II Classis (Double of the II Class)
Duplex Maius (Double Major)
Duplex (Minus) (Double (Minor))
Semiduplex (Semi-double)
Simplex (Simple)

The traditional system of ranking feasts comes from the rules for the recitation of the Divine Office. Feasts that are ranked *Duplex* or higher have their antiphons recited in full before and after the psalm. The feasts below the rank of the *Duplex* would not have their antiphons recited in full before the psalm. Instead, before the chanting of the psalm, only the incipit of the antiphon would be chanted. After the psalm, the antiphon would be sung in full. John XXIII changed the rubrics in 1960 so that the antiphon was always repeated in full before all psalms, no matter the ranking of the feast. This is one of the reasons why the ancient ranking of feasts was removed under John XXIII. Since the ranking systems are vastly different, it is almost impossible to make a direct comparison between John XXIII's and the ancient one.

MASS AND THE RANKING OF FEASTS

The following are general rules for Masses in the classical Roman rite, based on the rank of the feasts they celebrate:

Duplex

• One Collect is said unless there is a commemoration.
• Gloria and Credo are sung according to rubrics.

Semiduplex and Simplex

• Several Collects are to be made according to the rubrics.
• During octaves, the Mass of the octave is said unless there is a proper Mass (such as Sundays within an octave).

FEAST DAYS OF SAINTS SIGNIFICANTLY ALTERED

There was a reshuffling and re-organization of feasts in the 1960 "reforms" that led to the removal of longstanding allocated days in the Roman calendar. Below is a list of some of the festal changes.

Feast Days Removed from the Universal Calendar	• St. Peter's Chair in Rome (Jan 18) • Finding of the Holy Cross (May 3) • St. John Before the Latin Gate (May 6) • Apparition of St. Michael (May 8) • St. Leo II (Jul 3) • St. Anacletus (Jul 13), St. Peter in Chains (Aug 1) • Finding of St. Stephen (Aug 3) • Commemoration of St. Vitalis (Apr 28)
Feasts Days Moved	• St. Irenaeus (Jun 28 to Jul 3) • St. John Mary Vianney (Aug 9 to Aug 8)
Feasts Demoted to a Commemoration	• St. George (Apr 23) • Our Lady of Mt. Carmel (Jul 16) • St. Alexius (Jul 17) • SS Cyriacus, Largus, and Smaragdus (Aug • Impression of Stigmata of St. Francis (Sep 17) • SS Eustace and Companions (Sep 20) • Our Lady of Ransom (Sep 24) • St. Thomas of Canterbury (Dec 29) • St. Sylvester (Dec 31) • Seven Sorrows of Our Lady in Passiontide
Local Feasts Removed[5]	• The Espousals of the Blessed Virgin Mary to St. Joseph (Jan 23) • The Flight of Our Lord into Egypt (Feb 17) • The Prayer of Our Lord Jesus Christ (Tuesday after Septuagesima Sunday) • The Commemoration of the Passion of Our Lord (Tuesday after Sexagesima Sunday)

---

[5] In accordance with the February 1961 Instruction (§32, §33), fourteen feasts

Local Feasts Removed (cont.)	• The Holy Crown of Thorns (Friday after Ash Wednesday) • The Holy Lance and Nails (Friday after the I Sunday in Lent) • The Holy Shroud (Friday after the II Sunday in Lent) • The Five Wounds (Friday after the III Sunday in Lent) • The Most Precious Blood (Friday after the IV Sunday in Lent) • The Eucharistic Heart of Jesus (Thursday after the Octave of Corpus Christi) • The Humility of the Blessed Virgin Mary (Jul 17) • The Purity of the Blessed Virgin Mary (Oct 16) • The Translation of the House of the Blessed Virgin Mary (Dec 10) • The Expectation of the Blessed Virgin Mary (Dec 18)

The removal of numerous traditional feasts from the liturgical calendar is detrimental to the spiritual well-being of the faithful, as it strips them of welcome opportunities to engage deeply with the truths of the Faith. Pope Pius XI in *Quas Primas* deals specifically with the importance of feasts in the life of the faithful:

> For people are instructed in the truths of faith, and brought to appreciate the inner joys of religion far more effectually by the annual celebration of our sacred mysteries than by any official pronouncement of the teaching of the Church. Such pronouncements usually reach only a few and the more learned among the faithful; feasts reach them all; the former speak but once, the latter speak every year — in fact, forever. The Church's teaching affects the mind primarily; her feasts affect both mind and heart, and have a salutary effect upon the whole of man's nature. Man is composed of body and soul, and he needs these external festivities so that the sacred rites, in all their beauty and variety, may stimulate him to drink more deeply of the fountain of God's teaching, that he may make it a part of himself, and use it with profit for his spiritual life.[6]

What did the traditional missal look like before the reforms of the 1960s?

---

observed in local calendars were suppressed unless "truly special reasons" required their continued observance (see *AAS 53* [1961]: 174, www.vatican.va/archive/aas/documents/AAS-53-1961-ocr.pdf).

[6] Pius XI, *Quas Primas*, December 11, 1925, www.vatican.va/content/pius-xi/en/encyclicals/documents/hf_p-xi_enc_11121925_quas-primas.html.

SUNDAYS

The ranking of Sundays is split into the "Greater Sundays" and the "Lesser Sundays." Greater Sundays are split into I and II Classes.

Greater Sundays of the I Class are the first Sunday of Advent, the four Sundays of Lent, Passion Sunday, Palm Sunday, Easter Sunday, Low Sunday, and Pentecost. These cannot be trumped by any feast. The Greater Sundays of the II Class are all the other Sundays of Advent and the three Sundays before the beginning of Lent. These are trumped by any feast of the rank of *Duplex I Classis*. All other Sundays are known as Lesser Sundays and are trumped only by feasts that are *Duplex I* or *II Classis*.

FERIAS

Ferias have a different ranking system in the pre-1960 rubrics.

• Greater Privileged Ferias are ferial days that can never be impeded. These are Ash Wednesday and Monday, Tuesday, and Wednesday of Holy Week. No feast day could be celebrated on these days.

• Greater Non-privileged Ferias are ferias that hold the rank of *Simplex*. These are the ferias of Advent, Lent, Passion Week, Rogation Monday, and the Ember Days.

OCTAVES

The first day of an octave is called the feast day, the last day of an octave is called the "octave day," and the days in between are called "days within the octave." The ranking of these days varies depending on the type of octave. There are three ranks of octaves: Privileged, Common, and Simple.

Privileged octaves came in three ranks. The first rank includes those whose feasts cannot be trumped for the entire octave. The octaves of Easter and Pentecost are of this rank. The second rank of privileged octaves includes Epiphany and Corpus Christi. The octave days are *Duplex Maius*, and the days within the octave are semi-doubles, being displaced only by feasts of the *Duplex I Classis*. The third rank of privileged octaves includes Christmas, Ascension, and Sacred Heart. Days within such octaves are trumped by any feast over the *Simplex*.

The first type of non-privileged octave is the "common octave." The feasts that have a common octave are the Immaculate Conception, the Assumption, the Nativity of Saint John the Baptist, the

Solemnity of St. Joseph, the feasts of Saints Peter and Paul, All Saints, and the principal patron saint of a church, cathedral, order, town, diocese, province, or nation. The days within the octave are *Simplex*.

The last type of octave is the "simple octave." This pertains to the feasts of Saint Stephen, Saint John the Evangelist, Holy Innocents, Saint Lawrence, the Nativity of the Blessed Virgin, and secondary patrons. The feast days themselves are *Duplex II Classis*, the octave day is a *Simplex*, and no days within the octave are commemorated.

ST. JOSEPH IS NOT MENTIONED IN THE *CANON MISSAE*

John XXIII decreed on November 13, 1962 that the name of St. Joseph should be added to the Canon of the Mass after the name of the Blessed Virgin. Missals were starting to be published before this decree, which means that it may be possible to celebrate according to the 1962 missal without the name of St. Joseph in the Canon. The decree, however, came into effect on December 8 of the same year.

The primary objection to the insertion of St. Joseph into the *Canon Missae* is that the Canon had remained mostly untouched since antiquity. Pope Benedict XIV remarked with pride that no pope had added to the *Canon Missae* since Pope St. Gregory the Great (540–604).[7] St. Gregory compiled what he had at the time and introduced the phrase "*diesque nostros in tua pace disponas*" into the *Hanc igitur*. While the principal concern is thus the rupture with tradition, it is also necessary to consider the rationale behind this addition — namely, that the inclusion of St. Joseph was intended as a liturgical monument to the Second Vatican Council and its fruits (see *Decretum* in the *Acta*, November 13, 1962), a point which some likewise regard as problematic.[8]

THE USE OF THE BIRETTA

At the start of Mass, it is common in most places that the celebrant processes to the altar while wearing a biretta. Places that have friars or monks will sometimes see the celebrant wearing a hood or capuce in place of the biretta. This is of ancient origin and the reason the amice is first touched to the head before being

---

[7] Fortescue, *The Mass*, 172.
[8] For more on this topic, see Peter Kwasniewski, "On the Insertion of St Joseph's Name into the Roman Canon," *New Liturgical Movement*, December 23, 2019.

worn around the shoulders and neck. The origin of the removal of the biretta for Mass comes from the 1962 *Missale Romanum*.

Before the 1962 edition, the *Ritus Servandus* had always stated:

> Sacerdos, omnibus paramentis indutus, accipit manu sinistra Calicem, ut supra praeparatum, quem portat elevatum ante pectus, Bursam manu dextera super Calicem tenens, et facta reverentia Cruci, vel imagini illi, quae in Sacristia erit, capite cooperto accedit ad Altare, ministro cum Missali et aliis ad celebrandum necessariis (nisi ante fuerint praeparata) praecedente, superpelliceum induto.

> The priest, vested in all the vestments, takes the Chalice, prepared as above, with his left hand, which he carries elevated before his chest, holding the Burse with his right hand over the Chalice, and, having made a reverence to the Cross, or to that image which will be in the Sacristy, with his head covered, he proceeds to the Altar, preceded by the minister, who is vested in a surplice, carrying the missal and other things necessary for the celebration (unless they have been prepared beforehand).

However, in the 1962 Roman Missal, one finds the following:

> Sacerdos, omnibus paramentis indutus, accipit manu sinistra calicem, ut supra praeparatum, quem portat elevatum ante pectus, bursam manu dextera super calicem tenens, et facta reverentia Cruci, vel imagini illi, quae in Sacristia erit, accedit ad altare, ministro cum missali et aliis ad celebrandum necessariis (nisi ante fuerint praeparata) praecedente, superpelliceum induto.

> The priest, vested in all the vestments, takes the chalice, prepared as above, with his left hand, which he carries elevated before his chest, holding the burse with his right hand over the chalice, and, having made a reverence to the Cross, or to that image which will be in the Sacristy, he proceeds to the altar, preceded by the minister, who is vested in a surplice, carrying the Missal and other things necessary for the celebration (unless they have been prepared beforehand).

The complete omission of the phrase "with the covered head" is interpreted by most to mean that the use of the biretta is not required at Mass and, therefore, should be omitted. However, some rubricists stress that this is a relaxation and not a ban on the biretta. On the contrary, most tend to interpret the omission in the text as meaning the omission of the biretta for Mass.

THE PROPER LAST GOSPEL

The custom of reciting the prologue of the Gospel of St. John at the end of every Mass originated in the Middle Ages as a private devotional exercise for the priest; but since the people believed that these words constituted a powerful blessing, they wished to hear them said in their presence ("over them," in a certain sense); hence, the last gospel merged with the end of the Mass, a position it definitively obtained in the missal of St. Pius V. In subsequent centuries, the custom developed of replacing the prologue with the gospel of the day if another higher-ranking observance had supplanted it. Thus, before the Pacellian reforms of 1955, the "space" of the last gospel was utilized either to continue the commemoration of a saint that was begun in the orations, or, when a saint's feast superseded a Sunday, Vigil, or Lenten feria, to make room for the gospel that had been "missed." An example of this would be if St. Michael were to land on a Sunday, then the Michaelmas was celebrated, with the Last Gospel being the Gospel of the Sunday. In this way, the Sunday is commemorated by a Collect, Secret, Postcommunion, and Gospel. Another example of a Proper Last Gospel would be on the third Mass of Christmas. Because the Gospel of the Mass is John 1:1–14, the missal says that the Gospel of Epiphany is said in place of the Last Gospel. A liturgical ordo is quite handy in that it will point out when the Last Gospel changes.

BOWS TOWARDS THE CRUCIFIX

The rubrics for the missal of 1962 omit the line that says that some bows are made to the crucifix rather than to the book. This includes bows when uttering the Holy Name of Jesus (which is found mostly in the conclusions of the prayers), the *Gloria Patri*, and the name of a saint on the saint's feast day. The traditional rule is that at any mention of the Holy Name and the first half of the *Gloria Patri*, the celebrant is to bow towards the altar cross. There are also other bows towards the cross at a Trinitarian formula, but the *Gloria Patri* is the most common. At any mention of Our Lady or saints on their feast day, a bow is made towards an image of the saint if it is set above the altar. If not, a bow to the book is made. All liturgists interpret this omission as a simple bow to the book instead of the traditional bow to the altar crucifix or image. The classical missal of the Roman rite mentions it as follows:

> Cum nominatur nomen JESUS, caput versus Crucem inclinat: quod etiam facit cum nominátur in Epistola. Et similiter ubicumque nominatur nomen B. Mariæ, vel Sanctorum de quibus dicitur Missa, vel fit Commemoratio: item in Oratione pro Papa, quando nominátur, semper caput inclinat, non tamen versus Crucem; nisi in loco principali Altaris habeatur simulacrum vel imago B. M. V. aut Sancti, ad quam caput inclinatur. Si plures Orationes sint dicendæ, idem in eis, in voce, extensione manuum, et capitis inclinatione, quod supra dictum est, observatur.

> When the name of JESUS is mentioned, he bows his head towards the Cross; which he also does when it is mentioned in the Epistle. And likewise, wherever the name of the Blessed Mary or of the Saints of whom the Mass is being said or who are being commemorated is mentioned; likewise, in the Prayer for the Pope, when he is named, he always bows his head, but not towards the Cross, unless in the principal place of the Altar there is an image or statue of the Blessed Virgin Mary or of the Saint, towards which the head is inclined. If multiple Prayers are to be said, the same is observed in them regarding the voice, the extension of the hands, and the inclination of the head, as stated above.

Conversely, the missal of John XXIII states the following:

> Cum in oratione, vel alibi in Missa, pronuntiatur nomen IESU vel MARIAE, itemque cum exprimitur nomen Sancti vel Beati de quo dicitur Missa aut fit commemoratio, vel Summi Pontificis, sacerdos caput inclinat. Si plures orationes sint dicendae, idem in eis, in voce, extensione manuum, et capitis inclinatione, quod supra dictum est, observatur.

> When in the prayer or elsewhere in the Mass the name of JESUS or MARY is pronounced, likewise when the name of the Saint or Blessed of whom the Mass is being said or who is being commemorated, or of the Supreme Pontiff, is expressed, the priest bows his head. If multiple prayers are to be said, the same is observed in them

regarding the voice, the extension of the hands, and the inclination of the head, as stated above.

CONFITEOR BEFORE THE COMMUNION OF THE FAITHFUL

In the missal of John XXIII, the Confiteor before Holy Communion was removed, at least in grades of Mass lower than Solemn. However, it did remain in the *Pontificale Romanum* in force in the same year. This practice, like others mentioned above, remains commonplace in Masses celebrated today according to the missal of 1962, but it should be omitted if one is to follow strictly the rubrics of the same book. In the classical Roman rite, the Confiteor is to be sung at Solemn Masses by the deacon and recited by the servers at Sung and Low Masses.

In the *Missale Romanum* of 1920, the Confiteor before Holy Communion can be seen:

> Si qui sunt communicandi in Missa, Sacerdos post sumptionem Sanguinis, antequam se purificet, facta genuflexione, ponat particulas consecratas in Pyxide, vel, si pauci sint communicandi, super Patenam, nisi a principio positae fuerint in Pyxide seu alio Calice. Interim minister ante eos extendit linteum seu velum album, et pro eis facit Confessionem dicens: *Confiteor Deo*, etc. Tum Sacerdos iterum genuflectit, et manibus junctis vertens se ad populum in cornu Evangelii, dicit: *Misereátur vestri*, et *Indulgéntiam, absolutiónem, et remissiónem peccatórum vestrórum*, etc., et manu dextera facit signum crucis super eos. Postea genuflectens, accipit manu sinistra Pyxidem seu Patenam cum Sacramento, dextera vero sumit unam particulam, quam inter pollicem et indicem tenet aliquantulum elevatam super Pyxidem seu Patenam, et conversus ad communicandos in medio Altaris, dicit: *Ecce Agnus Dei, ecce, qui tollit peccáta mundi*. Deinde dicit: *Dómine, non sum dignus, ut intres sub tectum meum, sed tantum dic verbo, et sanábitur ánima mea*.

> If there are any to receive Communion during the Mass, the Priest, after consuming the Blood and before purifying himself, having made a genuflection, places the consecrated particles in the Pyx, or, if only a few are to receive, on the Paten, unless they had been placed from the beginning in the Pyx or in another Chalice. Meanwhile, the

minister spreads a linen cloth or white veil before them and recites the Confession on their behalf, saying: *I confess to Almighty God*, etc. Then the priest genuflects again and, with hands joined, turning toward the people at the Gospel corner, says: *May Almighty God have mercy on you* . . . and May *He grant you Pardon, absolution, and remission of your sins*, etc., making the sign of the cross over them with his right hand. Afterward, genuflecting, he takes the Pyx or Paten with the Sacrament in his left hand, and with his right hand takes one particle, which he holds slightly elevated between his thumb and index finger over the Pyx or Paten, and, turning toward those receiving Communion at the centre of the Altar, he says: *Behold the Lamb of God, behold Him who takes away the sins of the world*. Then he says: *Lord, I am not worthy that You should enter under my roof, but only say the word, and my soul shall be healed.*

Regarding the same rite, the *Missale Romanum* of 1962 states:

> Si qui sum communicandi in Missa, paulo antea ministrans campanulas signo eos moneat. Sacerdos autem, post sumptionem Sanguinis, calicem parum ad latus Evangelii collocat, intra tamen corporate, et palla tegit. Deinde, si particular super corporate consecratae sint, facta genuflexione, eas super patenam ponit; si particulae in eadem Missa intra pyxidem consecratae sunt, pyxidem collocat in medio corporali, earn discooperit et genuflectit; si vero administrandae sunt particulae iam antea consecratae, aperto tabernaculo, genuflectit, pyxidem extrahit et discooperit. Postea accipit manu sinistra pyxidem seu patenam cum Sacramento, dextera vero sumit unam particulam, quam inter pollicem et indicem tenet aliquantulum elevatam super pyxidem seu patenam, et, conversus ad communicandos in medio altaris, dicit: *Ecce Agnus Dei, ecce qui tollit peccata mundi.* Deinde dicit: *Domine, non sum dignus, ut intres sub tectum meum, sed tantum die verbo, et sanabitur anima mea.*

If there are any to receive Communion during the Mass, the minister shall give them a signal with the small bell shortly beforehand. The priest, however, after consuming the Blood, places the chalice slightly towards the Gospel side, yet still within the corporal, and covers it with the pall. Then, if particles have been consecrated on the corporal, after making a genuflection, he places them on the paten; if the particles have been consecrated in the same Mass within the pyx, he places the pyx in the middle of the corporal, uncovers it, and genuflects; but if the particles to be distributed have been previously consecrated, upon opening the tabernacle, he genuflects, takes out the pyx, and uncovers it. Then, he takes the pyx or paten with the Sacrament in his left hand, while with his right hand he takes one particle, which he holds slightly elevated between his thumb and index finger over the pyx or paten, and, turning toward those to receive Communion at the centre of the altar, he says: *Behold the Lamb of God, behold Him who takes away the sins of the world.* Then he says: *Lord, I am not worthy that You should enter under my roof, but only say the word, and my soul shall be healed.*

THE SANCTUS CANDLE

The Sanctus candle is the name given to a small candle that is placed on the epistle side of the altar in between the tabernacle and the Low Mass candle on that side. The Sanctus candle is lit at the Sanctus and extinguished at the end of the ablutions.

Although the use of a Sanctus candle is often neglected, it is still found in the rubrics of the 1962 Roman Missal[9] and mentioned by most liturgical commentators.[10]

The Sanctus candle is not used at Solemn Masses as the torchbearers are present. It is a widespread practice that at Sung Masses, where there are no torchbearers, the Sanctus candle is lit at the usual time and in the usual manner. However, in places where the custom has never existed, one is not obliged to have the Sanctus candle.

WHAT SHOULD WE MAKE OF THE 1962 MISSAL?

The 1962 missal represents a departure from the classical Roman rite in a strict sense. While the Tridentine Mass underwent various adjustments between 1570 and 1962, the distinct rubrical changes introduced from 1960 to 1962 marked a significant break from the earlier tradition. There were some reasons as to why John XXIII thought it would be best to create these rubrics. These reasons

---

[9] *Rubricae Generales Missalis Romani* 20.
[10] Fortescue, *Ceremonies of the Roman Rite*, 79; Josephus F. van der Stappen, *Sacra Liturgia* (H. Dessain, 1904), 101.

include that some of the rubrics had fallen into disuse and that the additions of Pius X seemed oddly placed at the end of the first section of the missal. This new set of rubrics also allowed incorporation of the major rubrical reforms of 1955 and 1960. Despite this, however, John XXIII kept *Quo Primum* at the head of the missal, along with the other bulls of his predecessors, still believing he was bound by them. Is the missal of 1962 still the classical Roman rite? Yes, but just barely. While it retains the core structure and essential prayers of the traditional Roman rite, the significant rubrical modifications—particularly those affecting the calendar, the ranking of feasts, and the rubrics of the Mass—mark a clear departure from its earlier form.

The simplification of the rubrics of the missal was received by some well, and by others not so well. Rarely can one see in today's world a Mass celebrated purely according to the missal of John XXIII. We still see such practices as bowing to the crucifix and the Confiteor prior to the distribution of Holy Communion, which were abolished by John XXIII but are still the norm in most places. Even looking at footage from the period, one can see that these instructions were not followed. In Ushaw College, a key seminary in England with the priority of instructing future priests in the most correct and devout celebration of Mass and the sacraments, one can see that things such as the recitation of the epistle by the celebrant at Solemn Mass and the deacon's Confiteor are still kept. It seems that at the time, most were "picking and choosing" which parts of the decree they should follow. The logic for this conservatism was that these ceremonies are supported by immemorial custom, something which cannot be removed by the stroke of a pen and, therefore, can still be done.

THE 1964 USAGE OF THE 1962 MISSAL

Some may think that the 1964 reforms created a "missal of 1964." This is true to the extent that there were missals published in 1964 that featured changes purportedly inspired by the Council. However, no new edition of the missal was officially released by the Vatican; hence, one is better off regarding the 1964 stage as nothing other than a usage of the 1962 missal. Indeed, publishers were rather frantically creating and selling "updated" editions of missals during the whole period from 1962 to 1969, as the rubrics and rules changed almost yearly. While none of these can be called a new *editio* of the missal, strictly speaking, commentators often speak loosely of a missal of this or that year.[11]

The 1964 reforms, introduced under the notorious Consilium led by Cardinal Lercaro and Father Annibale Bugnini, represent a significant step towards the dismantling of the sacredness and unity of the Roman rite. Under the guise of promoting active participation, the use of the vernacular was permitted—though one could argue it was more imposed than allowed—across numerous sacred parts of the Mass.

The proclamation of the Epistle and Gospel could be done solely in vernacular, rather than the sacred tongue of Latin, shattering centuries of liturgical unity and tradition. The chants of the Ordinary of the Mass, including the Kyrie, Gloria, Credo, Sanctus, and Agnus Dei, were subjected to the vulgar tongue, thereby stripping them of their ancient dignity and alienating the faithful from the universal language of the Church—simultaneously marginalizing the ancient melodies designated for use in the Mass. Even the Lord's Prayer, a prayer said in the solemn language of the Church, was reduced to the vernacular, as was the formula *Ecce Agnus Dei* before Communion. The chants of the Proper of the Mass—the Introit, Gradual, Offertory, and Communion—were likewise thrown into the fray, along with the acclamations, greetings, and dialogues between the celebrant and the faithful, turning sacred dialogue into banal conversation. The missal of 1964 was the first to add to the *Ordo Missae* the rite of distributing Communion to the faithful, another departure from tradition. The beautiful formula for the distribution of Holy Communion, "May the Body of Our Lord Jesus Christ preserve your soul unto life eternal," was changed to "Body of Christ. Amen." Also worth noting is that some publishers began to publish the missal without *Quo Primum* and even without the rubrics and instructions. It was a period of freefall.

The introduction of Common Prayer or the "Prayer of the Faithful"[12] in the vernacular, without any mention of these prayers in the rubrics of the Order of Mass, only adds to the confusion and liturgical rupture. Moreover, this 1964 missal is a peculiar document. Published hastily before the comprehensive 1965 revisions, it retains the rubrics of the 1962 *Missale Romanum* but opens the

---

[11] The 1965 revisions to the *Ordo Missae* came into effect on Ash Wednesday of 1965; the 1967 revisions came into effect June 29, 1967.

[12] This notion is mentioned in *Sacrosanctum Concilium* 53.

floodgates to the use of the vernacular, creating a disjointed and awkward liturgical rite. It is telling that where these vernacular options are printed, there is no Latin alternative presented, hinting at the Consilium's true intention: to begin the steady erasure of Latin from the Mass altogether. For example, the language used in a decree sent from the Consilium (Prot. n. 622/24) to the bishops of the United States of America, *linguam anglicanam adhibere licet* ("it is permitted to use the English language"),[13] ostensibly grants a permission, yet the decree as a whole reads more as a mandate to discard the sacred language of the Church in favor of the vulgar.

Also, concelebration was permitted, and the Sacred Congregation of Rites published the new liturgical norms in the document *Inter Oecumenici*, which detailed some of the changes. "On Sundays and on the other greater holydays a sung Mass shall be celebrated, with all who live in the house participating; there is to be a homily and, as far as possible, all who are not priests shall receive communion. Once the new rite has been published, concelebration is permitted for priests, especially on more solemn feasts, if pastoral needs do not require individual celebration."[14] At some stage, concelebration was limited to having twelve priests, mirroring the apostles. Concelebration of Mass had always existed in the West, but not in this manner. A newly ordained priest and a newly consecrated bishop concelebrate their first Masses in their roles. This involves kneeling a little away from the altar and reciting most of the prayers of the celebrant. This new instruction from the Congregation of Rites seems to have implied the need for the priests themselves to determine how they would implement these changes. What could go wrong? The missal of 1965 later clarified that any priest might concelebrate as long as he could see the altar at which Mass was being celebrated.

Thus, the 1964 reforms marked a deliberate move toward desacralization through the changes mentioned above, sowing seeds of discord and confusion that would soon culminate in the full-scale liturgical upheaval of the post-Vatican II era.

---

[13] *Roman Missal* (Catholic Book Publishing Co., 1964), 6; The Saint Bede Studio, "Anglophone Missals of the 'Interim Rite' 1964–1969: I," December 16, 2014, https://saintbedestudio.blogspot.com/2014/12/anglophone-missals-of-interim-rite-1964.html.

[14] Consilium, "*Inter Oecumenici*—Instruction on Implementing Liturgical Norms," *Adoremus*, September 26, 1964, https://adoremus.org/1964/09/inter-oecumenici/, 15.

THE 1965 MISSAL

The 1965 missal, often heralded as the "actual Mass" of Vatican II, serves as a glaring example of how the liturgy was reshaped under the guise of "modest" reform, while laying the groundwork for the radical upheavals that were to follow. This missal, introduced amidst a whirlwind of changes, sought to merge the traditional structure with modern innovations that only succeeded in stripping the Mass of its dignity. The prayers at the foot of the altar, once a deep and contemplative preparation for the sacred mysteries, were gutted—Psalm 42 was reduced to a mere antiphon, mirroring the usage of the Requiem Mass. Though still retaining the Confiteor, the shift to the vernacular, a language of the profane, weakened the unifying power of Latin that had echoed within sacred walls for centuries.

The 1965 missal also opened the door for the celebrant to recite the Gloria, Creed, and other prayers in the vernacular, encouraging a cacophony of voices and diminishing the solemnity of the Mass. The Mass of the Catechumens now allowed for the celebrant to sit passively while a lay lector read the Epistle in the common tongue, a departure from the traditional roles and dignity of the ordained ministers. The Prayers of the Faithful were resurrected not as the solemn intercessions of old[15] but as optional and locally fabricated add-ons, further undermining the sacred liturgy. Although the Canon remained, the 1965 missal left the door ajar for more drastic alterations—multiple signs of the cross were eliminated, the celebrant could face the people during parts of the Mass, and the introduction of newly crafted prefaces foreshadowed the impending chaos. The Last Gospel, a cherished conclusion that had graced the Mass for centuries, was unceremoniously omitted, silencing the proclamation of Christ's Incarnation.

Though its innovations were modest compared to those of the 1969 missal, the 1965 missal subtly deconstructed cherished and characteristic elements of the Roman rite, allowing the "hermeneutic of discontinuity" to burgeon and fester. This so-called "bridge" to reform was, in truth, a bridge to liturgical rupture, a harbinger of the disintegration of sacred tradition in favor of modernism's reckless experimentation. To no one's surprise, the binding document of *Quo Primum* was, for the first time, not to be found in the missal

---

[15] Such as with the intercessions of Good Friday.

of 1965, thus ending the almost 400-year legacy of Pius V.[16] The changes in this missal, while appearing conservative, were indeed the beginnings of a liturgical winter whose chill is still felt today.

Prelates offer the Holy Sacrifice in 1966: concelebrating *versus populum* at a freestanding altar (of boomerang design).

Concelebration according to the 1965 Roman Missal.[17]

---

[16] One may jest and say that *Traditionis Custodes* refers neither to the missal of 1962 nor to the missal of the classical Roman rite, but rather the 1965 missal simply because it uses the term "the missal antecedent to the reform of 1970."
[17] Shawn Tribe, "The History and Forms of the Christian Altar: The Twentieth Century to Present," *Liturgical Arts Journal*, May 5, 2023, www.liturgicalartsjournal.com/2023/05/the-history-and-forms-of-christian.html.

7

Instaurare Omnia in Christo

HERE DO WE GO FROM HERE? WHAT do we do? What does the future look like? These are all the critical issues within the minds of those concerned with the liturgy and the survival of the Church. However, to navigate the future well, it is essential that we look to the traditions of the past.

THE PERIOD AFTER THE COUNCIL

Let us look at the "glory days of the Church," that being the period directly after the Second Vatican Council. What was the most common form of the traditional Mass celebrated by those who held dear to the Catholic faith in those desperate times? The answer is complex. There were constant debates over whether the missal of 1920, 1955, 1962, 1964, or 1965 should be celebrated. The English mostly kept to the Mass before the changes of Pope Pius XII (including Holy Week). We can see this in the actions of people such as Fr. Montgomery Wright, who worked tirelessly for the care of souls in the period after the council using the traditional rites of the Church. The Americans mostly stuck to the use of the 1962 missal.[1] The French (save the Society of St. Pius X) used the 1964 missal. However, these are over-simplifications. There was no uniform, universal approach to the *Missale Romanum*. Due to the crisis that had occurred, there were many opinions about which edition to use.

What about in Rome? Abbé Franck Quoëx was one of the most renowned and skilled masters of ceremonies. He was originally part of the Institute of Christ the King Sovereign Priest (ICRSS) when they formed and later left to teach liturgy at one of the famous Roman universities. A majority of the solemn liturgies publicly celebrated in Rome were organized and executed under his guidance. These were celebrated according to the pre-Pius XII

---

[1] What Catholics Believe, "Why Does SSPX Use the 1962 Missal?," October 28, 2023, www.youtube.com/watch?v=h_esB7bqioU&ab_channel=What-CatholicsBelieve-Highlights.

ceremonies. Ceremonies such as the Mass of the Presanctified and the Ember Days were carried out with such precision and devotion that it was difficult to find any fault. The folded chasubles that had been thrown into the back of cupboards were restored and used for the sacred mysteries. The ICRSS also provided the faithful with the use of the ancient rites, which one can see in pictures from Gricigliano, the Institute's seminary in Italy, at the time.

So why did the 1962 missal come to dominate the traditional movement? Why did it become mainstream? The answer is simply because the Society of St. Pius X (SSPX) chose it as their baseline. Archbishop Lefebvre founded the SSPX in response to the atrocities committed against the Faith in the 1970s. Though quite old, he seemed to be the only one who would be able to pass on the torch of the Catholic faith to younger men desirous of becoming priests. In the early days of the seminary, any of the traditional missals was allowed. One can even see pictures of Marcel Lefebvre concelebrating according to the Mass of 1964![2] Also allowed were a range of views regarding the seat of St. Peter. The common factor that bound everyone there was the truth of Catholic doctrine. The purpose of the SSPX was to keep the Faith; in the words of Lefebvre, based on those of St. Paul: *Tradidi quod et accepi* ("I delivered unto you that which I have received"). The SSPX was there to keep intact the doctrine of the Church and see that it was not abandoned, as well as to labor for the salvation of souls. However, when Archbishop Lefebvre first sought to impose the 1962 missal, particularly at the North American Seminary, he was met with resistance by nine members in the form of a letter (and later a meeting) in which they cited problems regarding the See of Peter's vacancy and the content of the 1962 missal. The Nine were expelled from the SSPX in April 1983. It is worth noting that in 1976, Lefebvre held a meeting in Écône where it was decided that the SSPX missions in Europe and America were allowed to use the pre-Pius XII rubrics for the celebration of Mass and the Office.[3]

It would seem that Lefebvre honed his defense of the 1962 missal reactively as he dealt with the aftermath of the Nine. In a

---

[2] This was with Fr. Franz Schmidberger, on October 24, 1982, in Germany.
[3] MHT Seminary, "Questions for the Rector | Ep. 31: Bishop Richard N. Williamson," February 26, 2025, www.youtube.com/watch?v=57dUrYBs964&ab_channel=MHTSeminary.

letter to the SSPX dated April 24, 1983, he articulated his stance
in such a way as to exclude both the *Novus Ordo* and the pre-1955
rite.[4] As the late Fr. Gregory Hesse used to say, if one were to
shout at you on the street, you do not have the right to pull out
a gun and shoot him immediately. However, if one were to have
you at gunpoint, you would be able to draw a weapon. This is the
general rule of self-defense that the Archbishop applied to the
liturgy. With this logic, Lefebvre chose the 1962 missal, as it was
the last acceptable missal in his mind. It contained *Quo Primum*
and can still be seen as a descendant of the classical Roman rite.
This reasoning is apparent in Archbishop Lefebvre's letter in 1983,
which states that he follows

> the principle taught by St. Thomas Aquinas in the *Summa
> Theologica* (II, II, q. 33, a.4)—that one may not oppose
> the authority of the Church except in the case of immi-
> nent danger to the Faith. Now, there is no danger for
> the Faith in the liturgy of Pope Pius XII and Pope John
> XXIII, whereas there is great danger for the Faith in the
> liturgy of Pope Paul VI, which is unacceptable.

He also wrote in 1988 that "in order that uniformity might prevail in the Society, we decided to hold to the 1962 edition as well
as to its calendar, since we consider the advantages to be greater
than the disadvantages . . . " However, despite saying that there
was "no danger to the Faith" while admitting that the missal of
1962 had "disadvantages,"[5] Archbishop Lefebvre still kept many

---

[4] The history of Lefebvre and the Nine is quite complex. See "The Letter of
'The Nine' to Archbishop Lefebvre," March 25, 1983, www.traditionalmass.
org/images/articles/NineLetter.pdf; the 1982 and 1983 talks given by Marcel
Lefebvre to the Ridgefield seminarians, in typescript at https://archive.org/
details/LefebvreRidgefield8283A/; Anthony Cekada, "The Nine vs. Lefebvre: We Resist You to Your Face" (2008), www.traditionalmass.org/images/
articles/NineVLefebvre.pdf. According to Fr. Jenkins, SSPV, "Why Does
SSPX Use the 1962 Missal?" (www.youtube.com/watch?v=h_esB7bqioU),
the insistence on the '62 began not with the missal but with the breviary,
under the argument that unity was needed when members of the SSPX met
to pray in common—with the archbishop's assurance that this rule would
apply only to the office, not to the missal. If he is correct, the '62ization of
the SSPX was incremental.
[5] Marcel Lefebvre, "Letter to American Friends & Benefactors" (April 28,
1983), cited in Nicholas Mary, "Matters Arising: Why Does the Society Use
the Missal of 1962?," Great Britain Society of Saint Pius X, https://fsspx.
uk/en/matters-arising-why-does-society-use-missal-1962-35683.

things that John XXIII suppressed with his new code of rubrics, such as bowing to the cross for the Holy Name, the Confiteor before Communion, and, in some places, the changing of the termination of hymns according to the season. While he may simply have been acting from habit, it is also possible Archbishop Lefebvre thought that these attempted "reforms" were too much of a departure from tradition and thus decided to keep the earlier practice.[6] But on what basis? Why have a schizophrenic liturgy? Why not be consistent instead of making your own rules? There should be no rite of Écône, nor a rite of Gricigliano. We need the *Roman* rite as it was codified at Trent for the edification of souls. It simply does not make sense to "pick and choose." We often condemn "cafeteria Catholics" for selecting doctrines. We should look at ourselves and rectify this seductive fault, so characteristic of the modern world. Let us embrace "a form of liturgy handed down and received, whole and entire, as a rule of faith and law of life."[7]

LIVING IN A POST-BENEDICT XVI WORLD

Summorum Pontificum was released in 2007 and explained the right of every priest within the Church to celebrate Mass using the missal of 1962, without any permission required. Why the choice of the 1962 missal? Because it was already in common use by the clergy of the SSPX and FSSP, two of the larger traditionalist groups. However, not much later, the Holy See allowed for the celebration of the pre-Pius XII Holy Week rites. The Holy See recognized that there was much demand for these rites. People had come to understand the negative consequences of the Pius XII reforms and saw that the way forward, for the good of the Church and the salvation of souls, was the authentic Roman rite of Holy Week. It was victory for those in the Church who believed they needed such "permission."

---

[6] It is worth noting that the FSSP, being somewhat of an offshoot from the SSPX, kept the 1962 missal with some pre-1962 ceremonies. It can be said that Archbishop Lefebvre was not in favor of restoring the pre-1962 books as he saw nothing in the 1962 Roman Missal that was contrary to the Faith. The reason why he rejected the *Novus Ordo Missae* was due to his viewing it as dangerous to the Faith. But we have highlighted the fact that he was not a "1962 purist." This was shown by his mixing of elements and ceremonies between the 1962 and pre-1962 Roman missals.

[7] Peter Kwasniewski, *Close the Workshop: Why the Old Mass Isn't Broken and the New Mass Can't Be Fixed* (Angelico Press, 2025), 109.

While permission was given only to certain groups of pontifical rite, these Holy Week ceremonies were celebrated in churches that had no connections to the FSSP, ICRSS, or IBP (Institute of the Good Shepherd). Even diocesan Latin Mass parishes were celebrating these ancient rites. Did they get in trouble? No. No one saw the need for them to be corrected. There were no decrees from Rome, no censures, no letters, no worries or concerns. The Holy See, or at least the Pontifical Commission *Ecclesia Dei* (PCED) and bishops, knew what was occurring but did not find it necessary to rebuke. Those who applied for permission from Rome to celebrate the Tridentine ceremonies of Holy Week were given temporary permission almost instantly. The tides were turning. The missal of the classical Roman rite, seen as permitted in perpetuity by *Quo Primum* and the various popes who solemnly reiterated it, cannot be stopped or suppressed.

The Holy See also published a universal Ordo for those celebrating the missal of John XXIII. This Ordo was published all the way to a 2021 edition; the release of *Traditionis Custodes* in July of that year presumably undermined whatever draft might have been in process for 2022 at the time. These ordos started off as "strictly 1962." However, slowly, older elements were added. First came the *Benedicamus Domino* as the dismissal in times when there was no Gloria. Then came the introduction of octaves, such as that of Corpus Christi, for the benefit of the faithful. We can see that there was a desire, coming from the Holy See itself, for the reintroduction and re-establishment of the classical Roman rite. In a sense, the 1962 missal was becoming once again a transitional missal — this time, in the direction of the classical Roman rite!

However, under the pontificate of Francis, PCED was absorbed into the then Congregation for the Doctrine of the Faith (CDF). Peter Kwasniewski, in chapter 12 of his book *The Once and Future Roman Rite*, argues that the developments concerning the pre-1955 Holy Week represent a significant shift towards reclaiming the Church's ancient liturgical practices, without requiring explicit permission from Rome for everyone or in every circumstance. Drawing parallels between the Jews' return from the Babylonian exile and the Catholic Church's gradual restoration of traditional liturgies, Kwasniewski sees the current moment as a turning point after seventy years of "liturgical exile." He contends that the Vatican's tacit acceptance of pre-1955 Holy Week celebrations, without expressly granting permission in every case, reflects an understanding that these older forms are immemorially sacred and great. This suggests that Catholics do not need to wait for approval from ecclesiastical authorities to celebrate what has always been a core part of their spiritual heritage; these traditions carry their justification within themselves. He criticizes the notion that venerable customs must be defended in a "court of law" when they have already stood the test of centuries as the "received and approved rites" praised by the Council of Trent (Sess. VII, can. 13) and the *Professio fidei Tridentina* or Creed of Pius IV. Much like the Jews' longing for true worship upon returning to Jerusalem, Catholics are now reclaiming their liturgical heritage with renewed zeal, confident in the legitimacy of their actions. This grassroots revival will continue to grow, revitalizing the Church's liturgical life as more communities recognize the inherent rights of immemorial custom and move beyond scruples about needing explicit permission. The belief in a need for ad hoc permission rests on a misunderstanding, or rather, a gross underestimation, of the authority that resides in the venerable rites we have inherited.

WHY TRY TO "REVIVE" THE PRE-1962 MISSAL?

The 1962 missal is indeed the Mass of Pius V in its essence, as evidenced by the inclusion of *Quo Primum* and its general alignment with the Tridentine missal, and it significantly expresses the traditional faith while maintaining a connection to the perennial liturgical practices of the Roman tradition. However, it is not the most authentic expression of the Roman rite, as the alterations made to it demonstrate, and there is a distinction between a liturgy that merely expresses the Faith and one that also embodies the continuity of liturgical practice. An entirely new liturgy, created *ex nihilo*, might theoretically articulate the Faith just as effectively — or even more so — than the 1954 missal, but it would lack the vital thread of liturgical continuity.[8] By shifting the

---

[8] This is a critical weakness in the arguments advanced by Archbishop Lefebvre, who equated the "traditional Mass" primarily with a Mass that *expresses the traditional faith* rather than one that maintains *unbroken continuity with the liturgical past.* This oversight, or blind spot, must be recognized and addressed if we are to engage in a more comprehensive and meaningful discussion about the evaluation, and consequent acceptance or rejection, of liturgical changes. Indeed, the argument that certain papal actions may

discussion to this broader and more principled ground, we can better appreciate the importance of both doctrinal fidelity *and* liturgical continuity in preserving the integrity of the Roman rite. This is not to suggest that the 1962 missal should be dismissed or boycotted; it remains a valid and grace-filled expression of the traditional faith. Nevertheless, it represents a slight departure from the fuller liturgical authenticity found in earlier missals, and this nuanced perspective is essential for a deeper understanding of the Roman rite's development and preservation.

Rather than rejecting the 1962 missal outright, it would be more constructive to encourage those who celebrate it to explore and incorporate elements from the pre-1962 liturgical tradition.[9] This could include restoring abolished feast days (often found in the Masses for Diverse Places section of the 1962 missal), reintroducing the Confiteor before Communion, and the priest's reciting the Epistle and Gospel at the altar during Solemn Mass. Such steps would prepare the way for the full restoration of the Roman rite, allowing the faithful to gradually reconnect with its richer and more authentic expressions. By reintroducing these elements, the 1962 missal can act as a bridge, fostering a deeper appreciation for the liturgical heritage of the Church and paving the way for the eventual restoration of the Roman rite in its fullness.

In practical terms, the reintroduction of the pre-1962 liturgy may likely go unnoticed by the average layperson. However, with proper catechesis, the faithful could come to appreciate the depth and richness of the Roman rite, which the 1962 missal, as valuable as it is, does not fully embody. This approach respects both the continuity of liturgical practice and the integrity of the Faith it seeks to express.

ARGUMENTS FROM CANON LAW

Why should we consider the revival of the pre-1962 Roman liturgy when the missal of 1962 has long been what Michael Davies called a "rock of stability" for the traditional movement? The answer lies not in any hankering for variety but in the deeper,

---

have been *ultra vires*—outside of the scope of papal authority—offers a more robust and convincing framework for critiquing liturgical reforms than the narrower focus employed by Archbishop Lefebvre.

[9] See Appendix 3 for a thorough and practical guide to transitioning from 1962 to pre-1955, in regard to both the Mass and the Office.

unyielding principles of ecclesiastical law and custom. The classical Roman rite, firmly rooted in the practices established at the
Council of Trent and sanctified by the decrees of Pope St. Pius
V, has never been fully abrogated in a manner that would render
it obsolete. When discussing the legal framework within which
the old rite can be revived, it is crucial to distinguish between
"abrogation" and "reprobation" in canon law.[10] For instance,
while Pope Pius X explicitly suppressed the old Roman psalter
in his *Divino Afflatu* reform, subsequent liturgical reforms did
not openly repeal the existing forms — they simply introduced
new ones with the expectation that the clergy would adapt. Thus,
the older rites remain administratively suppressed rather than
reprobated, meaning their use does not violate divine law and
can be reinstated under proper circumstances.

Canon law, particularly as codified in the 1983 *Codex Iuris Can-*
onici, permits the continuation or revival of immemorial customs
that meet specific conditions. For a custom to be valid, it must
not violate divine law, it must be capable of being received by
a community of faithful under its proper legislative authority,
and it must be stable and intentionally practiced. The old liturgy,
having been practiced for over a millennium and embodying
both textual and practical continuity, meets these criteria. The
legitimacy of reviving such customs finds strong grounding in
the principles articulated by St. Thomas Aquinas in his *Summa*
theologiæ[11] and by St. Augustine, who observed that the customs
of God's people and the institutions of our ancestors should be
regarded as laws.[12] Aquinas further elaborates that repeated external actions, aligned with the deliberate judgment of reason, can
establish customs that hold the force of law. This demonstrates
that liturgical norms evolve organically through sustained practice,
rather than by arbitrary imposition.

Evidence for this can be seen in the assertion that the Tridentine liturgy, defined as the Roman rite codified at Trent and used

---

[10] In canon law, abrogation means the complete repeal of a law, removing
its legal force (though not its revivability), while reprobation refers to
the formal condemnation of a custom or practice in such a way that it is
excluded from any possibility of legitimate revival.

[11] *Summa theologiæ* I-II, Q. 97, art. 3.

[12] Letter 54 *ad Januarium*. Also worth noting is the maxim of Ivo of Chartres:
"Mos populi Dei et instituta maiorum pro lege tenenda sunt." (The customs
of God's people and the institutions of our ancestors are to be held as law.)

until (and possibly not including) John XXIII, was sanctioned by an ecumenical council and a binding papal decree and built upon ancient custom crystallized according to the highest standards of Church law—namely, general magisterial assent and papal judgment in unison. This reinforces its status as a reasonable and practical option for revival. Canon law, like a rulebook for sacred matters, needs to be understood within its practical and pastoral context. Before *Summorum Pontificum*, it was possible to access the older liturgies through available missals and reprints, demonstrating their accessibility and feasibility without excessive effort or reliance on obscure medieval sources.

Moreover, the 1983 Code's nuanced distinction between abrogated and reprobated customs is crucial. Abrogated customs, suppressed by legislative decree, can be revived under certain conditions, whereas reprobated customs—those inherently violating divine law or morals—cannot. John Beal, in his *New Commentary on the Code of Canon Law*,[13] clarifies that "reprobated" customs, which are forbidden, differ from "abrogated" customs that were administratively suppressed but can be legitimized again. The classical Divine Office, for example, although contrary to modern liturgical norms, enjoys the highest state of approval possible, that of a pope in union with an ecumenical council. Therefore, the revival of the old liturgy, if done as a stable and intentional practice by a legitimate authority, aligns with both canonical and historical principles. Canon law also recognizes its authority as stemming from longstanding customs. Before the codification of law, both custom and canon were understood as protective and proscriptive, not merely prescriptive. This outlook remains embedded in Church doctrine, explicitly reaffirmed in the letter *Con Grande Fiducia* that accompanied *Summorum Pontificum*, which declared: "What earlier generations held as sacred remains sacred and great for us too, and it cannot be all of a sudden entirely forbidden or even considered harmful." These liturgies are not historical artefacts but legitimate forms of worship that have persisted and shaped the Faith over centuries.

From this, we see that while modern reforms have introduced new practices, the older ones retain a strong legal, spiritual, and pastoral basis for revival, especially where communities of the

---

[13] Paulist Press, 2000, p. 84.

faithful seek to adopt them under their proper ecclesiastical authority. This balance between tradition and contemporary pastoral needs underscores the timeless relevance of the pre-1962 Roman liturgy within the broader life of the Church.

ANALYSIS OF SPECIFIC CANONS[14]

Canon 23–28: Customs in Canon Law

Can. 23: Only that custom introduced by a community of the faithful and approved by the legislator according to the norm of the following canons has the force of law.

Can. 24 § 1: No custom which is contrary to divine law can obtain the force of law.

§ 2: A custom contrary to or beyond canon law (*praeter ius canonicum*) cannot obtain the force of law unless it is reasonable; a custom which is expressly reprobated in the law, however, is not reasonable.

Can. 25: No custom obtains the force of law unless it has been observed with the intention of introducing a law by a community capable at least of receiving law.

Can. 26: Unless the competent legislator has specifically approved it, a custom contrary to the canon law now in force or one beyond a canonical law (*praeter legem canonicum*) obtains the force of law only if it has been legitimately observed for thirty continuous and complete years. Only a centenary or immemorial custom, however, can prevail against a canonical law which contains a clause prohibiting future customs.

Can. 27: Custom is the best interpreter of laws.

Can. 28: Without prejudice to the prescript of can. 5, a contrary custom or law revokes a custom which is contrary to or beyond the law (*praeter legem*). Unless it makes express mention of them, however, a law does not revoke centenary or immemorial customs, nor does a universal law revoke particular customs.

Canons 23 and 26 establish that custom can acquire the force of law when it is longstanding and approved by legitimate authority,

---

[14] *Code of Canon Law*, accessed March 4, 2025, https://www.vatican.va/archive/cod-iuris-canonici/cic_index_en.html.

with canon 24 §1 affirming that the custom must be reasonable and not contrary to divine law. The authentic Roman liturgy, having been practiced uninterrupted for over a millennium, clearly qualifies as an immemorial custom. To dismiss the value of such an ancient and deeply rooted tradition would be to undermine the principles enshrined in canon law, which protects and recognizes longstanding customs. The classical Roman rite, formally approved by Pope St. Pius V and the magisterium, remains a legally and spiritually significant form of worship. Under canons 23–28, the pre-1962 rites, far from being obsolete, retain their legal viability and should be restored, with proper ecclesiastical oversight, as they offer a profound link to the Church's rich liturgical heritage.

Canon 27 declares that custom is the best interpreter of laws, providing a solid argument for the restoration of the authentic Roman rite. The centuries of practice of the traditional liturgy serve not only as an expression of custom but also as a guide to understanding the Church's liturgical law. St. Basil the Great, writing in the fourth century, stressed that the unwritten customs of Church liturgy, even though not based on direct commands of the scripture, nevertheless transmit the teaching of the Church "in a mystery," passed from the apostles in such a form as to protect the dignity of the dogma from profanation by those who could not fully understand it.[15] These words of St. Basil were received in the West through a paraphrase and included in the twelfth-century *Decretum* of canon lawyer Gratian.[16] Until the enactment of the 1917 Code, the *Decretum* possessed very high canonical authority in the Church, second only to papal legislation; the *Decretum* was given official publication by Pope Gregory XIII in 1582. The theological understanding of St. Thomas Aquinas[17] stresses that longstanding practices, such as the Roman rite, are essential in shaping the life of the Church. Modern liturgical reforms may have sought to address new pastoral needs, but the value of the Roman rite as an interpreter of liturgical law remains indisputable. Canon 27 supports the restoration of the older rites as an expression of continuity and a legitimate part

---

[15] St. Basil, *On the Holy Spirit*, ch. 27.

[16] Gratian, *Decretum*, Dist. 11, c. 5.

[17] "Custom has the force of law, abolishes law, and is the interpreter of law" (*Summa theologiæ* I-II, Q. 97, art. 3).

of the Church's tradition, without dismissing the importance of addressing contemporary concerns; indeed, such restoration is arguably among the most timely of all responses to the post-modern crisis of meaning and identity.

While it is true that legal customs typically govern interpersonal relationships, the Church's canonical tradition has long recognized that liturgical practices, though primarily concerned with the relationship between the faithful and the divine, also fall under the jurisdiction of canon law. The inclusion of liturgical norms within the legal framework of the Church highlights their dual role: as acts of worship and as expressions of the Church's juridical order. Canon 27's assertion that "custom is the best interpreter of laws" affirms that longstanding liturgical customs indicate a legal continuity that complements their theological significance. Furthermore, while modern legal theory may distinguish between legal and liturgical customs, the Church's tradition does not separate them. The immemorial Roman rite, therefore, serves not only as a theological beacon but also as a normative guide within canon law. The preservation of these rites safeguards both the spiritual and legal heritage of the Church.

Canon 846 §1, Canon 2, and Canon 5 §1: Laws and Decrees Regarding the Liturgy

> Can. 846 §1: In celebrating the sacraments the liturgical books approved by competent authority are to be observed faithfully; accordingly, no one is to add, omit, or alter anything in them on one's own authority.
>
> §2: The minister is to celebrate the sacraments according to the minister's own rite.
>
> Can. 2: For the most part the Code does not define the rites which must be observed in celebrating liturgical actions. Therefore, liturgical laws in force until now retain their force unless one of them is contrary to the canons of the Code.
>
> Can. 5 §1: Universal or particular customs presently in force which are contrary to the prescripts of these canons and are reprobated by the canons of this Code are absolutely suppressed and are not permitted to revive in the future. Other contrary customs are also considered

suppressed unless the Code expressly provides otherwise
or unless they are centenary or immemorial customs
which can be tolerated if, in the judgment of the ordinary, they cannot be removed due to the circumstances
of places and persons.

Canon 846 §1 states that the liturgical books must be faithfully observed, which some may interpret as requiring exclusive
adherence to post-Vatican II liturgical texts. However, canon 2
clarifies that older rites, unless explicitly abrogated, retain their
force. Importantly, similar canons could be found in the old
Code of Canon Law of 1917, canons 2 and 733. Canon 733[18] §2
contained the word "nevertheless" (*autem*) before the provision
that the minister must follow his own rite, which contrasts this
provision with the preceding section that prescribes the faithful
observance of the liturgical books. This suggests that the Code
admitted the existence of different versions of approved liturgical
books within one rite, rather than only one set of books. Canon
6 §2 of the current Code of Canon Law provides that, in so far as
the canons of the Code repeat older law, they must be assessed in
accordance with canonical tradition. From this it follows that the
current Code, just like the previous Code, allows the existence
of different versions of approved liturgical books.[19] Hence, the
classical Roman rite, which has never been formally abrogated or
suppressed by any explicit legislative act of the Holy See, retains its
legal standing within the Church. This is confirmed by the principle of canon 2 of the 1983 Code, which preserves liturgical laws in
force prior to the code unless they are explicitly contradicted by

---

[18] "Can. 733. §1: In Sacramentis conficiendis, administrandis ac suscipiendis
accurate serventur ritus et caeremoniae quae in libris ritualibus ab Ecclesia
probatis praecipiuntur. §2: Unusquisque autem ritum suum sequatur, salvo
praescripto can. 851, § 2, 866." (§1: In the confecting, administering, and
receiving of the Sacraments, the rites and ceremonies prescribed in the ritual
books approved by the Church must be carefully observed. §2: However,
each one is to follow his own rite, without prejudice to the prescriptions
of can. 851, §2, and 866.)

[19] Benedict XVI recognized that multiple books may exist in the same rite
in *Summorum Pontificum*, arriving at the "useful (legal) fiction" that there
are two "forms" of one rite (the term "form" had never been used in an
official sense like this; it appears to be his own conceptualization). Thus,
one can see that multiple approved books can exist at the same time for
diverse communities. See Gregory DiPippo, "The Legal Achievement of
Summorum Pontificum," *New Liturgical Movement*, July 5, 2017.

its provisions. Furthermore, the absence of any universal decree revoking the pre-1962 liturgical books, coupled with the Church's historical practice of preserving liturgical diversity, underscores the continued legitimacy of the traditional liturgy. While modern reforms have introduced new liturgical forms, they do not inherently invalidate or abolish the older rites, particularly when a community of faithful seeks to maintain this form of worship in accordance with canonical tradition.[20]

Canon 5 § 1 makes a key distinction between customs that have been explicitly abrogated and those that remain in force unless directly annulled. The pre-1955 Roman liturgy, while administratively suppressed, was never formally abrogated and, crucially, was never reprobated as contrary to divine law.[21] This distinction allows the Roman rite to be "revived," given that it was not (and indeed could not be) condemned or invalidated by the Church. Canon 5 supports the idea that the older liturgy, with its deep roots in the Church's history, can and should be restored under appropriate circumstances. Far from being a relic of the past, the Roman rite represents a timeless form of worship that continues to hold a legitimate place within the Church's liturgical life. The authentic rites of the classical Roman rite should be reinstated as a living tradition that speaks to the spiritual needs of many Catholics.

Canon 135 §2, Canon 838 §1 and 2:
Authority and Legislative Power

> Can. 135 § 2: Legislative power must be exercised in the manner prescribed by law; that which a legislator below the supreme authority possesses in the Church cannot be validly delegated unless the law explicitly provides otherwise. A lower legislator cannot validly issue a law contrary to higher law.

> Can. 838 § 1: The direction of the sacred liturgy depends solely on the authority of the Church which resides in the Apostolic See and, according to the norm of law, the diocesan bishop.

---

[20] For further argumentation that this remains the case even after *Traditionis Custodes*, see the sources mentioned in note 24 below.

[21] This is especially true if we remember that canon 2 provides that the Code, as such, does not define the rules of liturgy or intend to change them.

§ 2: It is for the Apostolic See to order the sacred liturgy of the universal Church, publish liturgical books and review their translations in vernacular languages, and exercise vigilance that liturgical regulations are observed faithfully everywhere.

Canon 135 § 2 affirms that the legislative authority of the pope and ecumenical councils holds primacy in creating and modifying Church laws, including liturgical regulations. However, this authority is exercised for the common good, a principle that extends to safeguarding the Church's spiritual and liturgical heritage.[22] Canon 838 § 1–2 further clarifies that the Apostolic See retains ultimate responsibility for the sacred liturgy. Papal documents such as *Quo Primum* and *Quod a Nobis* emphasize that the Roman rite, codified after the Council of Trent, was not merely established as a legislative norm but was also intended to serve as a unifying standard for liturgical practice and doctrinal fidelity. For instance, *Quo Primum* explicitly states that the missal promulgated by Pius V was to remain in perpetuity, ensuring that no one could "ever be forced to abandon this missal," thereby underscoring its role in preserving liturgical unity and continuity with tradition. One can see in *Quod a Nobis* the desire for the common good, as Pius V disliked that "each bishop made himself a particular breviary, thus tearing, so to speak, by means of these new offices, dissimilar and proper, for each diocese, this communion which consists in offering to the same God prayers and praises in the one and same form."[23] The preservation of the liturgical books of the classical Roman rite serves the common good by providing continuity with the Church's bimillenial tradition, guarding doxological sacredness and confessional identity.

The enduring significance of the older rites has not been eclipsed by subsequent modern liturgical developments.[24] Many

---

[22] See Peter Kwasniewski, *Bound by Truth: Authority, Obedience, Tradition, and the Common Good* (Angelico Press, 2023).

[23] *Quod a Nobis* 1. For the full text, see Appendix 4.

[24] Regarding the postconciliar liturgical reform, some authors maintain that Paul VI did not have the authority to make the number and nature of changes he made to the liturgy; others maintain that he would have had authority only to place his new rite *alongside* the old rite; still others, that he never formally promulgated the new rite in such a way as to abrogate the old rite and mandate the new — which was the view arrived at by the

authors argue that immemorial liturgical tradition, universally received and approved by the Church over centuries, possesses an inherent primacy of honor and a duty of usage. This tradition binds all members of the Church, including the hierarchy, to revere it and faithfully hand it on.[25] The Roman Rite, as codified by St. Pius V in *Quo Primum* and defended in *Quod a Nobis*, preserves liturgical unity and doctrinal clarity in a form of worship organically developed under the guidance of Divine Providence and made venerable with the weight of ages. Building on this, many scholars have contended that the newer liturgical forms introduced in the twentieth century did not, and indeed could not, abrogate the traditional rites. This view was affirmed by the 1986 commission of cardinals[26] and later articulated by Benedict XVI in *Summorum Pontificum*. Restoring the Roman Rite in its fullness thus serves the common good by ensuring continuity with tradition, protecting the domain of the sacred and transmitting the Faith through long-received and venerable forms of worship.

---

commission of cardinals in 1986 and eventually formulated by Benedict XVI in *Summorum Pontificum*. For further reading, see Peter Kwasniewski, "The Pope's Boundedness to Tradition as a Legislative Limit" and related essays by other authors in *From Benedict's Peace to Francis's War: Catholics Respond to the Motu Proprio "Traditionis Custodes" on the Latin Mass*, ed. idem (Angelico Press, 2021); Fr. Réginald-Marie Rivoire, F. S. V. F., *Does "Traditionis Custodes" Pass the Juridical Rationality Test? A Canonical-Theological Study* (Os Justi Press, 2022); Peter Kwasniewski, "Does a Priest Need Permission to Offer the Traditional Latin Mass?," *Tradition and Sanity Substack*, April 3, 2025.

[25] The Papal Coronation Oath, which has been unfortunately out of use for some time, consolidates the traditional understanding of this concept: "I shall keep inviolate the discipline and ritual of the Church just as I found and received it handed down by my predecessors [*disciplinam et ritum Ecclesiae, sicut inueni et a sanctis predecessoribus meis traditum repperi, inlibatum custodire*], and I shall preserve the Church's property undiminished and take care it is kept undiminished; I shall neither subtract nor change anything from the tradition my most esteemed predecessors have safeguarded and I have received, nor shall I admit any novelty, but shall fervently keep and venerate with all my strength all that I find handed down as verily my predecessors' disciple and follower; but if anything should come about contrary to canonical discipline, I shall correct it, and guard the sacred canons and constitutions of our pontiffs as divine and heavenly mandates, knowing that at the divine Judgment I shall render a strict account of all that I profess . . ." For the full text, see Kwasniewski, "Pope's Boundedness," 227–28.

[26] See Peter Kwasniewski, "Minutes from the Commission of Cardinals That Advised John Paul II to Lift Restrictions on the Old Missal," *New Liturgical Movement*, January 9, 2023.

Canon 20: Revival of Suppressed Customs

> Can. 20: A later law abrogates, or derogates from, an
> earlier law if it states so expressly, is directly contrary
> to it, or completely reorders the entire matter of the
> earlier law. A universal law, however, in no way derogates
> from a particular or special law unless the law expressly
> provides otherwise.

Canon 20 stipulates that an older law remains in effect
unless it is explicitly abrogated by a newer one.[27] The pre-Pius
XII Roman liturgy was never formally abrogated and, as such,
continues to hold a legal status within the Church. While
some might argue that the introduction of the new liturgy was
intended to replace the old, canon 20 clarifies that unless the
older rites were specifically revoked, they remain licit. This provides a strong legal foundation for the restoration of the Roman
rite, which continues to resonate with the spiritual needs of
many faithful. Its reinstatement would not only respect canon
law, but also serve to reinvigorate a crucial element of the
Church's sacred traditions.

"What earlier generations held as sacred, remains sacred and
great for us too, and it cannot be all of a sudden entirely forbidden
or even considered harmful" (*Summorum Pontificum*).

Canon 87 §1: Application of Canon Law and Dispensation

> Can. 87 § 1: A diocesan bishop, whenever he judges that
> it contributes to their spiritual good, is able to dispense
> the faithful from universal and particular disciplinary
> laws issued for his territory or his subjects by the supreme
> authority of the Church. He is not able to dispense, how-
> ever, from procedural or penal laws nor from those whose
> dispensation is specially reserved to the Apostolic See or
> some other authority.

Canon 87 § 1 grants bishops the authority to dispense
from certain disciplinary laws for the spiritual good of their

---

[27] This is a precise parallel to canon 22 of the 1917 Code: "A later law, laid
down by the competent authority, [abrogates] a prior law if it expressly says
so, or if it is directly contrary to it, or if it completely reorders the matter
treated in the earlier law; but, and though observing canon 6, n. 1, general
laws in no way derogate from the special [laws] of places and from the statutes
of [inferior authorities], unless expressly established otherwise in the law."

community. This provides bishops with the flexibility to restore the traditional Roman rite in areas where there is a clear pastoral demand. The use of the pre-1955 liturgy, far from creating division, can serve the spiritual well-being of the faithful, offering a form of worship that has sustained the Church and her saints for centuries. While ensuring that unity within the Church is preserved, canon 87 encourages bishops to recognize the enduring spiritual value of the older rites and thus to honor the deep liturgical heritage of the Church, for the benefit of the faithful who avail themselves of its abundance. It is worth noting that canon 87 was a new rule, first introduced by the 1983 Code of Canon Law, intended to establish a reasonable degree of decentralization in the Church and avoid the pitfalls of excessive centralism and hyperpapalism.

* * *

In conclusion, canon law provides a nuanced framework that supports the revival of the pre-1962 Roman liturgy while recognizing the legitimacy of post-Vatican II reforms. The balance between tradition and modernity, authority and custom, is delicately managed within these canons, allowing for the preservation of the old, provided that it serves the spiritual needs of the faithful under proper ecclesiastical authority.

ARGUMENT FROM LOGIC

According to those who were in charge of the liturgical reforms from 1948 onwards, the reforms under Pius XII were seen as a transition to something better to come (in this case, the *Novus Ordo Missae*).

The argument that the liturgical reforms under Pope Pius XII were transitional in nature is supported by several statements made by Bugnini, who was at the heart of the liturgical reform from 1948 until 1975. In his work *The Simplification of the Rubrics* (1955), Bugnini explicitly described the reforms as a temporary step, stating that they were "essentially a bridge between the old and the new,"[28] highlighting their contingent nature. He pointed out that the simplifications introduced at the time did not cover all aspects that warranted reform, but rather focused on "the

---

[28] Annibale Bugnini, *The Simplification of the Rubrics* (Doyle and Finegan, 1955), 19.

things that are easiest and most obvious"[29] in order to achieve immediate and tangible results.

Furthermore, Bugnini acknowledged that the reform process was just beginning, stating in his 1955 book that "this reform is only the first step toward measures of a wider scope."[30] This makes it clear that the changes in the 1950s were not intended to be the final word on liturgical practice but were part of a larger, phased transformation. He emphasized the inevitability of compromise in such a transitional phase, as the goal was to serve as a bridge between the existing liturgy and the broader reforms that would follow. This perspective was echoed in a 1956 commentary in *Bibliotheca Ephemerides Liturgicae*, where the new Holy Week rites introduced in 1955 were referred to as the "third step toward a general liturgical reform," reinforcing the idea that these changes were part of a longer process that culminated in later, more sweeping reforms.[31]

The transitional nature of the reforms is crucial in understanding why they are no longer to be considered binding. Laws within the Church, particularly those governing the liturgy, must possess the quality of stability or perpetuity to maintain their authority over time. However, from the very outset, the 1955 reforms under Pope Pius XII were described as temporary measures designed to serve as a stepping stone towards further developments. Bugnini himself repeatedly made it clear that the changes were not intended to be permanent fixtures but rather part of a larger, ongoing process of liturgical renewal. He referred to the reforms as a "bridge" and an "arrow indicating the direction taken by the current restoration," which indicates that the legislation was not set in stone but was subject to further evolution.

Given their lack of stability or permanence, it is unclear how these reforms could be considered lasting ecclesiastical law. Instead, they were designed to address immediate needs while paving the way for more substantial changes, as evidenced by the eventual introduction of the *Novus Ordo Missae* and the other liturgical books of Paul VI. In light of this, the reforms can be seen as provisional rather than definitive, meaning they were

---

[29] Bugnini, 21.
[30] Bugnini, 21.
[31] See the aforementioned address by Fr. Carlo Braga on the 1955 Holy Week Reform.

intended to be superseded by later developments. As such, their temporary nature undermines their ability to bind future generations, especially when the very purpose of the reforms was to initiate a broader reformation of the liturgy.

The reforms enacted under Pius XII were inherently transitional, lacking the qualities necessary for permanence, and thus do not hold the same enduring legal or liturgical weight as more definitive reforms. Their transitional nature supports the argument that traditionalists are justified in adhering to the pre-1955 rites, as the Pius XII reforms were never intended to serve as the final or unchanging form of the Roman liturgy. While the 1962 missal has received additional legal support since 1988, this does not negate the legitimacy of the older rites, which were never formally abrogated and retain their intrinsic value. The temporizing and transitory status of the Pius XII reforms, coupled with the enduring relevance of the pre-1955 liturgical tradition, underscores the continued validity and spiritual significance of the older forms of worship.

CONCLUSION

The way forward is not to treat these venerable traditions as anomalies but to integrate them into the life of the Church once more, respecting their deep roots and the sacred patrimony they represent and transmit. A community led by a bishop, abbot, or priest could legally revive these customs, fulfilling both the canonical requirements and the spiritual needs of the faithful. The revival of these rites would not be about indulging in nostalgia but about reclaiming a richer, more authentic worship experience that embodies the fullness of the Roman liturgical tradition as it has been lived for centuries. By reintroducing the classical Roman rite, the Church would be making a profound statement about continuity, fidelity, and the enduring sanctity of her liturgical life. The time is ripe for bishops, priests, and the faithful to embrace these traditions, ensuring that they once again become the living heartbeat of the Church's worship.

When will the Tridentine Rite be restored to its proper places in churches, cathedrals, and basilicas around the world? We simply do not know when. We know, however, that it *will* be restored. We see from the actions of the past three decades that PCED flirted with the idea. We even saw the Tridentine Rite offered in cathedrals, with cardinals and bishops present. The time to harvest is soon, but not yet. In the meantime, we should pray, fast, and endure penances until the time comes. With the arrival of a future pope who is authentically Catholic, we will see the restoration of all things in Christ: the liturgy, the breviary, the immemorial practices. Until then, "stand fast; and hold the traditions which you have learned" of the liturgy (2 Thess 2:14). Let us make the Tridentine Rite the highlight of our lives, living fruitfully according to its words and directions. Let us pave the path for future generations to hold on to what is sacred and cannot be abolished.

Mass of the Presanctified, ICRSS, Gricigliano, 2003.[32]

Abbé Franck Quoëx and Marcel Pérès assisting with the celebration of the Ember Days according to the authentic Roman rite sometime in the '80s or '90s in Rome.

---

[32] *The Rad Trad*, "Good Friday (Repost)," April 3, 2015, https://theradtrad. blogspot.com/2015/04/good-friday-repost.html.

8
Questions and Answers

ELOW FOLLOWS A BRIEF SUMMARY, IN question and answer format, of what has been explained in this book.

1. *Weren't the reforms of Holy Week in 1955 necessary?*

Far from being a "necessity," the 1955 reforms of Holy Week were a catastrophic rupture with the continuity of liturgical tradition. These changes, once again driven and guided by the 1948 Commission, stripped Holy Week of its depth and symbolism. Venerable rites that had survived centuries of persecution and upheaval were reduced to superficial ceremonies. The elimination of the *Missae Siccae* (Dry Masses) and the gutting of the Easter Vigil are just two examples of how the reforms mutilated the sacred liturgy. Good Friday, in particular, was massacred. What had been a solemn and mystical journey through Christ's Passion was reduced to a minimalist shadow of itself, comprising a "Liturgy of the Word" followed by a Communion service. Yes, one can argue that the times at which the liturgies would be celebrated had to be changed. However, the Tridentine rubrics themselves already indicate at least some of these times, which custom had gradually come to ignore. However, the change of times was made a pretext for many other innovations that paved the way for the tragic fall of the liturgy in the latter half of the twentieth century. The pre-1955 rites are preferable because they retain the solemnity and theological richness that have been lost in the name of so-called "pastoral accessibility" and "removing medieval accretions."

2. *Were the changes to the liturgical calendar and feast rankings in 1955 justifiable, given the need for simplification?*

The changes to the liturgical calendar and feast rankings in 1955 were not justifiable; they were an attack on the richness of the Church's liturgical life. By reducing vigils and octaves and abolishing certain feast rankings, the reforms sought to make the liturgy "easier" but instead robbed it of its depth and continuity. The traditional calendar had grown organically over centuries, reflecting the Church's deep understanding of the sacred rhythms of the liturgical year. The pre-1955 calendar maintained a connection to this heritage, while the post-1955 reforms severed that link, moving, abolishing, or curtailing many feast days and seasons of the year. The pre-1955 rites preserve the fullness of the Church's liturgical cycle, unbroken by rationalistic tampering.

3. Did Pius XII's reforms, particularly the reduction of the Eucharistic fast, promote a more accessible spirituality for the faithful?

Pius XII's reduction of the Eucharistic fast was a grave mistake that undermined centuries of spiritual discipline. The midnight fast had long been a means of preparing the soul to receive the Body of Christ, reflecting the seriousness and reverence with which the Eucharist should be approached. By reducing the fast, Pius XII weakened this sense of preparation, making it easier for the faithful to receive Communion without the necessary spiritual preparation. This was not a pastoral improvement; it was a capitulation to convenience. The pre-1955 fasting regulations preserved the sanctity of the Eucharist, encouraging the faithful to approach it with the reverence it demands.

4. Should the 1962 missal be viewed as a failure to preserve the true Roman rite, despite being labelled as "traditional?"

The 1962 missal is often mistakenly seen as the last authentic representation of the Roman rite, yet this missal was a product of dangerous compromises, influenced heavily by the 1948 Commission and Annibale Bugnini. Bugnini, who would later spearhead the creation of the *Novus Ordo*, was already sowing the seeds of disruption under Pius XII. The reforms leading to the 1962 missal represent a departure from the organic development of the liturgy, instead introducing unnecessary innovations that paved the way for further decay. The 1962 missal is a diluted, compromised version of what once was the Church's most sacred treasure.

5. Doesn't the 1962 missal at least preserve the core elements of the traditional Roman rite?

The 1962 missal might retain the outward appearance of the traditional Roman rite, but beneath the surface, it is rife with compromises and departures from tradition. The core elements of the Mass may remain, but the surrounding context—the prayers, the rubrics, the calendar—has been eroded. Pius XII's reforms, beginning with the 1948 Commission and culminating in the missals of 1962–1965, removed key components of the liturgy that had once reflected profound theological truths of the Faith. The Mass is not just a collection of words and actions; it is a coherent whole, where every part contributes to the expression of the sacred mysteries. The 1962 missal, by altering this balance, distorts the Roman rite. Only the pre-1955 rites preserve the liturgy in its full integrity.

6. *Can the 1962 missal be considered a legitimate expression of the Roman rite when it was so heavily influenced by Bugnini and the modernist agenda?*

The 1962 missal, tainted by the influence of Bugnini and his agenda, cannot be considered a legitimate and authentic expression of the Roman rite. The Consilium's fingerprints are all over this missal, from the gutted Holy Week to the simplified rubrics. Bugnini's involvement in the 1948 Commission and his later role in the creation of the *Novus Ordo* make it clear that his goal was not to preserve tradition, but to undermine it.[1] The 1962 missal, though preferable to what followed, is nonetheless compromised. The pre-1955 rites, free from Bugnini's interference, represent the true Roman rite, untainted by the modernist agenda that would later wreak havoc on the Church. This critique demonstrates how the 1955 and 1962 reforms, far from being legitimate adaptations, were destructive to the continuity and integrity of the Roman rite. Only the pre-1955 rites preserve the true depth, beauty, and sacredness of the liturgical tradition.

7. *Wasn't the widespread usage of the 1962 missal after the Council a necessary step in safeguarding the Latin Mass from the modernist reforms of the Consilium?*

The 1962 missal did not fully safeguard the Latin Mass; it compromised it. This missal was the offspring of meddling liturgists who had meager respect for the organic liturgical development that had been preserved through the centuries. By the time the 1962 missal was promulgated, the groundwork for the destruction of the traditional liturgy had already been laid. The authenticity

---

[1] It may be argued that even if their intention was not to undermine tradition per se, this resulted from what they were trying to accomplish.

of the liturgy is not just determined by what can express the Faith well. What determines the legitimacy of these rites is that they both express the Faith and preserve the prior usage — provided there are no abuses that have arisen. The changes in this missal, from the altered rubrics to the mangled Holy Week rites, were not about protecting tradition but about undermining it. We can see that some of the other reforms of the twentieth century also eroded the authenticity of the liturgy. The authentic traditional rites, on the other hand, remain untainted by these Pistoian influences and offer a far more faithful representation of the Roman rite.

8. Does the simplification of the rubrics in the 1962 missal represent a legitimate adaptation to contemporary needs?

Simplification is a word often used to mask the true nature of these reforms: spoliation. The changes to the rubrics introduced by the 1962 missal were not a legitimate adaptation but a deliberate attempt to break with the traditional form of worship. Under Bugnini's influence, these reforms reduced the liturgy to something more palatable to modern sensibilities, flattening down the complexity that had been cultivated over centuries to express the profound mysteries of the Faith. The 1962 missal was not about making the Mass easier for the faithful; it was about clearing the path for more radical changes. The traditional Roman rubrics, in contrast, are a reflection of a deeper understanding of the sacred, where every gesture, word, and movement has a purpose rooted in centuries of tradition.

9. Isn't the introduction of vernacular hymns and similar simplifications in the 1962 missal an improvement in that these promoted greater participation among the laity?

The further commendation of vernacular hymns and simplifications in the 1962 missal was not an improvement; it was a betrayal of the sacred nature of the liturgy. These innovations reduced the Mass to a form of entertainment, where the focus shifted from the sacred mysteries to superficial engagement. The idea that simplification promotes greater participation is a modernist fallacy. True participation is not about external involvement but about an interior union with the sacrifice of Christ. The pre-1955 rites foster this interior participation through their reverence, complexity, and solemnity. Simplification, as introduced in the 1962 missal, only serves to diminish the sacred, turning the Mass into something mundane.

10. *Can a cleric satisfy the canonical obligation to recite the Office using books prior to 1961?*

The current Code of Canon Law states in can. 276: *obligatione tenentur sacerdotes necnon diaconi ad presbyteratum aspirantes cotidie liturgiam horarum persolvendi secundum proprios et probatos liturgicos libros* ("priests, as well as deacons aspiring to the priesthood, are bound by the obligation to recite the Liturgy of the Hours daily according to the proper and approved liturgical books"). This is the only hint we see in canon law regarding what books can be used. This provision repeats almost verbatim canon 135 of the 1917 Code of Canon Law, which provided that the clerics in major orders were obliged to the daily and full recitation of the canonical hours according to the proper and approved liturgical books.[2] The key words here are *proprios* and *probatos*—proper and approved.

The term "proper" denotes the priest's Office in relation to him. A secular priest, unless he is a tertiary, cannot recite the Dominican Office. Nor can a Franciscan recite the Ambrosian Office. Apart from extenuating circumstances (e.g., he is a Benedictine oblate), a secular priest should recite the Roman Office, as this corresponds to the rite he is ordained to celebrate. "Approved" is quite a vague word in this canon. It simply means that the set of liturgical books has been approved by the Church as to being found to satisfy the obligation. The books promulgated by Pope St. Pius X and even those promulgated after the Council of Trent fulfill the conditions for being "approved for use." They are all approved by the Church: by the then-reigning pope as the legislator and by the Sacred Congregation of Rites as a competent agency for matters liturgical. This alone should be enough for a

---

[2] Can. 135: "Clerici, in maioribus ordinibus constituti, exceptis iis de quibus in can. 213, 214, tenentur obligatione quotidie horas canonicas integrerecitandi secundum proprios et probatos liturgicos libros." (Clerics constituted in major orders, except those mentioned in can. 213 and 214, are bound by the obligation to recite the canonical hours in full daily, according to their own approved liturgical books.) Canons 213–14 provided an exception for laicised clerics and those ordained against their will.

cleric to fulfil his obligation by using them. As such, any edition
of the Roman Breviary that has been formally approved by the
Church for use by the clergy—including those prior to the 1955
revisions—could meet the canonical requirement.

The aforesaid is confirmed by the history of papal legislation on
liturgy since the Council of Trent and, especially, since the Second
Vatican Council. The apostolic constitution *Laudis Canticum* by
Pope Paul VI (November 1, 1970), which officially promulgated
the Liturgy of the Hours, did not officially abolish the Roman
Breviary and did not make the Liturgy of the Hours universally
obligatory or in any way whatsoever universal for application.
All it did canonically was to offer the Liturgy of the Hours for
acceptance by episcopal conferences[3] and give express permission
to the clergy who experienced "grave difficulties"[4] with the new
Office to recite the *Breviarium Romanum* that was previously in
use. Does this permission suggest, *a contrario sensu*, that the Roman
Breviary was normally forbidden? No, this interpretation cannot
be adopted, because, according to canon 18 of the current Code
of Canon Law, the canonical laws that restrict the free exercise
of rights are subject to strict interpretation.[5] This means that
permission of one case cannot be interpreted as prohibition of

---

[3] "Statuimus autem, ut novus hic Liturgiae Horarum liber statim usurpari
possit atque in lucem editus fuerit. Episcopales interea Conferentiae edi-
tiones eiusdem liturgici operis lingua vernacula apparandas curent atque,
post datam a Sancta Sede approbationem seu confirmationem, diem defin-
iant, quo eaedem, sive ex toto sive ex parte, in usum recipi possint vel
debeant" (*Laudis Canticum*). (We decree, however, that this new book of
the Liturgy of the Hours may be used as soon as it has been published.
In the meantime, the Episcopal Conferences shall ensure that editions of
the same liturgical work are prepared in the vernacular language and, after
obtaining approval or confirmation from the Holy See, shall determine the
date on which they may or must be adopted, whether in whole or in part.)
[4] "Iis vero, qui, ob provectam aetatem vel ob peculiares causas, graves
experiuntur difficultates in novo Ordine servando, licet, de consensu sui
Ordinarii ac tantummodo in recitatione a solo peragenda, Breviarium
Romanum, quod antea in usu erat, sive ex toto sive ex parte retinere"
(*Laudis Canticum*). (However, those who, due to advanced age or particular
reasons, experience serious difficulties in following the new Order are permitted, with the consent of their Ordinary and only in private recitation,
to retain the Roman Breviary previously in use, either in whole or in part.)
[5] Can. 18: "Laws which establish a penalty, restrict the free exercise of
rights, or contain an exception from the law are subject to strict interpretation" (CIC, 1983).

another case. Therefore, the permission of *Laudis Canticum* to use the Roman Breviary in certain cases means that the clergy have a strict right to do it in such cases, even if their superiors do not like it. Moreover, according to canon 10 of the Code of Canon Law, the law has an invalidating or disqualifying effect only if it expressly says so.[6] From this it follows that praying the traditional Breviary cannot be considered non-fulfilling of the canonical obligation, seeing that there is no direct provision to that effect in *Laudis Canticum* or any other law whatsoever.

Laudis Canticum permits the use of the Roman Breviary under two conditions: that it be done with the consent of the cleric's Ordinary (i.e., in most cases, a diocesan bishop) and only in private recitation (*a solo*). Should both conditions be considered strictly necessary for the licit use of the traditional Breviary? The answer is no. The first reason is that such an interpretation would contradict the above-mentioned canon 18 of the Code of Canon Law. *Laudis Canticum* restricts the free exercise of rights by the clergy and, therefore, must be interpreted strictly (narrowly). The second reason is that such an interpretation would incapacitate the Ordinary, depriving him of the power to direct the sacred liturgy in his diocese. A diocesan bishop is the director, promoter, and guardian of the entire liturgical life in the church entrusted to him (Can 835 §1, Code 1983); together with the pope and according to the rules of law, in the bishop is vested the authority over the direction of sacred liturgy (Can 838 §1, Code 1983 as amended in 2017). Holding that the bishop can permit a cleric to recite the traditional Breviary only if it is done in private would effectually partially disqualify the bishop in his power to direct the diocese's liturgical life; it would invalidate his permission to recite the Roman Breviary publicly. This would contradict the above-mentioned canon 10 of the Code, that the law has an invalidating or disqualifying effect only if it expressly says so. Therefore, *Laudis Canticum* should be interpreted to the effect that the private recitation of the Roman Breviary *must*, by a general rule, be permitted by the cleric's Ordinary. *Laudis Canticum* urges the clerics to approach their Ordinaries for permission

---

[6] Can. 10: "Only those laws must be considered invalidating or disqualifying which expressly establish that an act is null or that a person is affected" (CIC, 1983).

in any case, and the Ordinary is to establish if there is indeed a "grave difficulty" in using the standard Liturgy of the Hours and a "peculiar reason" to use the traditional Breviary. If the reasons are established, the Ordinary *must* permit the cleric at least a private recitation of the Breviary. However, nothing prevents the Ordinary from allowing a public recitation, as well, if he sees it to be fitting for the spiritual life of his church.

It is worth noting that, unlike *Laudis Canticum*, previous apostolic constitutions that reformed the breviary did sometimes use the language of "abolition" and "prohibition" in respect of the previously used versions. The apostolic constitution *Quod a Nobis* by St. Pius V (July 9, 1568), which introduced the Tridentine Breviary, abolished "whatever other Breviaries, either older or protected by any privilege ... and any use of such by any churches, monasteries, convents, militias, orders and places of the world...,"[7] albeit with an exemption for religious orders that long possessed their own version of the office. In a similar way, the apostolic constitution *Divino Afflatu* by St. Pius X (November 1, 1911), introducing a new version of the Roman Breviary, "abolished and completely forbade" the use of the previous order of the psalter.[8] However, reading these provisions in the context of other parts of these constitutions allows us to understand the intention of the legislating popes in both cases. Neither Pius V nor Pius X were trying to ban the older forms as something harmful or to ensure full uniformity of liturgy by extirpating "non-standard" forms. Both constitutions were strictly obligatory only for the clergy who were already accustomed to following the breviary of the Roman Church: "those who by law or custom must say

---

[7] "Ac etiam abolemus quaecumque alia Breviaria, vel antiquiora, vel quovis privilegio munita, vel ab Episcopis in suis Dioecesibus pervulgata, omnemque illorum usum de omnibus orbis Ecclesiis, Monasteriis, Conventibus, Militiis, Ordinibus, et locis virorum et mulierum . . ." (*Quod a Nobis* 4). (And furthermore, we abolish all other Breviaries, whether older, granted by any privilege, or promulgated by Bishops in their Dioceses, and entirely prohibit their use in all Churches, Monasteries, Convents, Military Orders, Religious Orders, and places of men and women throughout the world...)

[8] "Psalterii ordinem, qualis in Breviario Romano hodie est, abolemus eiusque usum, inde a Kalendis Ianuariis anni millesimi nongentesimi decimi tertii, omnino interdicimus" (*Divino Afflatu*). (We abolish the order of the psalter as it exists in the Roman Breviary today and completely prohibit its use from the first day of January, 1913.)

or chant the Canonical Hours according to the custom and rite of the Roman Church"[9] or "all those who by office or custom fulfil the canonical Hours according to the Roman Breviary."[10] Neither constitution concerned those who were using any other kind of breviary, a non-Roman one; *Quod a Nobis* also made an exception for the forms of breviary older than 200 years, as is well known. The intention in both cases was to make sure that there was only one "Roman Breviary," not two or more competing forms, each pretending to be "authentically Roman."

It is notable that subsequent reforms of the Roman Breviary, such as *Cum Nostra Hac Aetate* (1955) of Pius XII and *Rubricarum Instructum* (1960) of John XXIII, no longer use the language of "abolishing" or "prohibiting" the older versions. *Rubricarum Instructum* only states that the older rubrics "lose their legal force" (*vigere cessant*), which refers to the obligatory character of the older rubrics, not to their spiritual value. Possibly, this is a sign that with time, the Apostolic See realized more and more that abolitions and prohibitions of the traditional forms of the liturgy were not canonically or theologically possible and that using such terms in ecclesiastical legislation would lead to confusion and even consternation among the clergy and the faithful. Seeing that now the older versions of the Roman Breviary no longer have an obligatory legal force, while the Liturgy of the Hours, as was mentioned above, was never made obligatory, but was only offered for acceptance, a cleric today can, in theory, satisfy his canonical obligation by reciting *any* of the older forms of Roman Breviary, provided it was approved by the Apostolic See at some point.

As a canonist explained to the author, *Quod a Nobis* and *Divino Afflatu* technically imposed the canonical obligation only on those clerics who were constrained by the official canonical sanctions/penalties for non-recitation. The canonical sanctions were codified

---

[9] "Quoscumque, qui Horas Canonicas ex more et ritu ipsius Romanae Ecclesiae, iure vel consuetudine dicere vel psallere debent" (*Quod a Nobis* 6). (All those who are bound by law or custom to recite or chant the Canonical Hours according to the usage and rite of the Roman Church.)

[10] "Ab omnibus et singulis, qui ex officio aut ex consuetudine Horas canonicas iuxta Breviarium Romanum, a S. Pio V editum et a Clemente VIII, Urbano VIII, Leone XIII recognitum, persolvunt" (*Divino Afflatu*). (By all and each who, by office or by custom, recite the canonical Hours according to the Roman Breviary, published by St. Pius V and revised by Clement VIII, Urban VIII, and Leo XIII.)

for the first time in the 1917 Code of Canon Law. The 1917 Code contained a sanction for the grave neglect of the obligatory ritual ceremonies by a cleric, canon 2378: "Clerici maiores qui in sacro ministerio ritus et caeremonias ab Ecclesia praescriptas graviter negligant et moniti sese non emendaverint, suspendantur pro diversa reatus gravitate." (Major clerics who seriously neglect the rites and ceremonies prescribed by the Church in their sacred ministry and, after being warned, do not amend themselves, shall be suspended according to the gravity of their offence.) The modern Code of Canon Law of 1983 no longer contains a penal article for similar offences. This means that non-recitation of the canonical hours (whatever the form) is no longer considered a canonical offence, *per se*. The obligation of recitation for the secular clergy may thus, at this time, be a matter of divine law alone, with no additional obligation added by the legislation of the Church. Therefore, there is no strictly obligatory form of canonical hours nowadays, which means one must recite the office but is free to choose among the approved forms that pertain to his rite.[11]

---

[11] See Appendix 1 for further discussion.

Do Priests or Religious Need Special Permission to Pray a Pre-55 Breviary?

PETER KWASNIEWSKI

N OCCASION, I RECEIVE AN EMAIL LIKE the following (in this case, from a seminarian): "Do you happen to know of any sources/authoritative references which you could point me to that explain why praying the Pre-55 Breviary definitely satisfies the canonical obligation for clerics or religious? As I am strongly desirous of the Pre-55 Liturgy, I wanted to check all my p's and q's." (The same question could be asked, *mutatis mutandis*, about taking up a pre-Pius X breviary as well.)

MY INITIAL VIEW

In the past, my standard line has been: There is no official statement that you can do this. If one can do it, it is because "what earlier generations held as sacred, remains sacred and great for us too, and it cannot be all of a sudden entirely forbidden or even considered harmful. It behooves all of us to preserve the riches which have developed in the Church's faith and prayer, and to give them their proper place."[1] It can be done because it is the Church's venerable and immemorial *lex orandi*. If you are confident that this is true, then you have sufficient certainty that by fulfilling the obligation as it was fulfilled by countless saints before you, you too are fulfilling it today, in a way that is supererogatory inasmuch as it goes above and beyond the minimum that is required by current law.

However, I thought it best to solicit a variety of opinions from experts. I will now share their responses. As you'll see, opinions differ, but a certain majority consensus emerges.

---

[1] Benedict XVI, *Con Grande Fiducia*, July 7, 2007.

EXPERT OPINION #1: SECULAR PRIEST FROM AN *ECCLESIA DEI* INSTITUTE

"I am a bit more cautious when it comes to using an older version of the Office than an older version of the Missal, because I see a distinction between, on the one hand, something being the public prayer of the Church and, on the other, something fulfilling a positive obligation imposed by the Church through the power of the keys.

"I would say that if one were to pray the Office using an older version, it would still be the public prayer of the Church. But because the obligation to recite the Divine Office and its binding under the pain of mortal sin is something produced by positive ecclesiastical law, if the requirements as set forth by the law are not fulfilled, then the penalty is incurred. This is different from the Missal as there is, in general, *no obligation* to celebrate Mass — an exception being if it is required for the faithful to fulfill an obligation of attendance. For example, I would say that if Pius X had decided that secular clergy or clergy with pastoral responsibilities were bound to recite only Lauds and Vespers, they would fulfill their obligation and avoid sin by doing so, while if they went beyond this, it would still be part of the public prayer of the Church, but supererogatory. If, however, such a cleric (in this hypothetical scenario) prayed every Hour of the day *except* Lauds and Vespers, it would seem that he had not fulfilled the obligation and would incur the penalty, even though all of the other Hours prayed would still be the prayer of the Church.

"Touching on this topic, 'Art. 9 § 3 of the Motu Proprio *Summorum Pontificum* gives clerics the faculty to use the *Breviarium Romanum* in effect in 1962, which is to be prayed entirely and in the Latin language' (*Universae ecclesiae*, 32). In other words, the obligation can be, and is, fulfilled by using the '62 Breviary. This does not really answer the question definitively, but it might help shape the direction the discussion might go and the points which need to be considered in answering the question."

EXPERT OPINION #2: BENEDICTINE MONK

"Would the praying of the pre-55 Breviary constitute a mortal sin if ecclesiastical discipline established that one must pray the 1962 Breviary? Frankly, I think this is the sort of positivist nonsense that got us into trouble in the first place.

"The promise at ordination is to *pray the Divine Office*. Period. The Paul VI Liturgy of the Hours is so edited and short that I do not know how someone could possibly incur sin by saying the John XXIII breviary instead, as it is much longer and more demanding. (Imaginary confession: 'Bless me, Father, for I have sinned. I have prayed 150 psalms in the Office this week rather than 62.25!') So too, the older versions are still more demanding. ('Bless me, Father, I have prayed the Octave of All Saints and enjoyed it! Can this really be a sin?') Give me a break!

"In the early days of the Ecclesia Dei Commission, Cardinal Mayer was asked by a priest for permission to say the old breviary. His response was that no permission was needed because it is longer than the Breviary of Paul VI. Enough said. So too, the policy of positivism falls, for now *Summorum Pontificum* is abrogated. The Missal of 1962 is mandated by *Summorum*; yet it and all its predecessors are forbidden by *Traditionis Custodes*. Et cetera. Are we supposed to change our liturgical and devotional life with each new pontificate? Come on!

"If a seminarian wishes to pray more, let us thank God and concern ourselves with those who don't pray the breviary at all."

MY RESPONSE TO THE MONK

I am in full agreement. Thank you for your rant. Really, we should say this: The obligation of the cleric or religious is to honor God by praying the Divine Office, consisting of the psalms and other texts. As long as he is doing this in a manner "received and approved," he is fulfilling that task.

However, it must be recognized that the stranglehold of legal positivism is very powerful, and St. Pius X mightily contributed to it with his over-the-top language when promulgating his own new breviary:

> Therefore, by the authority of these letters, We first of all abolish the order of the Psaltery as it is at present in the Roman Breviary, and We absolutely forbid the use of it after the 1st day of January of the year 1913. From that day in all the churches of secular and regular clergy, in the monasteries, orders, congregations and institutes of religious, by all and several who by office or custom recite the Canonical Hours according to the Roman

Breviary issued by St. Pius V and revised by Clement VIII, Urban VIII and Leo XIII, We order the religious observance of the new arrangement of the Psaltery in the form in which We have approved it and decreed its publication by the Vatican Printing Press. At the same time, We proclaim the penalties prescribed in law against all who fail in their office of reciting the Canonical Hours every day; all such are to know that they will not be satisfying this grave duty unless they use this Our disposition of the Psaltery.

We command, therefore, all the Patriarchs, Archbishops, Bishops, Abbots and other Prelates of the Church, not excepting even the Cardinal Archpriests of the Patriarchal Basilicas of the City, to take care to introduce at the appointed time into their respective dioceses, churches or monasteries, the Psaltery with the Rules and Rubrics as arranged by Us; and the Psaltery and these Rules and Rubrics We order to be also inviolately used and observed by all others who are under the obligation of reciting or chanting the Canonical Hours. In the meanwhile, it shall be lawful for everybody and for the chapters themselves, provided the majority of the chapter be in favor, to use duly the new order of the Psaltery immediately after its publication.

This We publish, declare, sanction, decreeing that these Our letters always are and shall be valid and effective, notwithstanding apostolic constitutions and ordinances, general and special, and everything else whatsoever to the contrary. Wherefore, let nobody infringe or temerariously oppose this page of Our abolition, revocation, permission, ordinance, precept, statue, indult, mandate and will. But if anybody shall presume to attempt this, let him know that he will incur the indignation of Almighty God, and of His Apostles, Saints Peter and Paul.

Given at Rome at St. Peter's in the year of the Incarnation of the Lord 1911, on November 1, the Feast of All Saints, in the ninth year of Our Pontificate.

So, it seems to me, there must be a *theological rationale* for maintaining that something like this decree is null and void from the get-go. Not that Pius X's breviary would thereby be invalidated or rendered illegal, but his attempt to prohibit all contrary customs no matter how venerable seems like it would have to be null and void, if we take seriously the concept of tradition and do not think it is totally subject to the will of the reigning pontiff (cf. Benedict XVI's comments about the limits of the pope's authority: "The Pope is not an absolute monarch whose thoughts and desires are law.... The Pope knows that in his important decisions, he is bound to the great community of faith of all times...," etc.). If Benedict XVI is right, then the "sacred and great" principle takes precedence over attempts to thwart it.

One may sympathize with the hesitation of clergy or religious to take the line: "I am expressly disobeying the dictate of Pope *N.* in doing what I'm doing, because it rests on deeper and better principles than his." One would, at very least, need *moral certainty* that one had properly understood the nature of the obligation owed to tradition in contrast with that owed to papal legislation. After this appendix was written, my attention was drawn to the potent canonical argument found at the end of chapter 8, to which I refer the reader. — PAK I am reminded here of an exchange at the trial of St. Thomas More: "What, More, you wish to be considered wiser and of better conscience than all the bishops and nobles of the realm?" To which More replied, "My lord, for one bishop of your opinion I have a hundred saints of mine; and for one parliament of yours, and God knows of what kind, I have all the General Councils for 1,000 years, and for one kingdom I have France and all the kingdoms of Christendom."

THE MONK'S REPLY

"Yes, moral certainty is what one needs. But that comes easily enough when positive law twists and turns back on itself every few years. Pius X was a little over-the-top on authority, perhaps understandably so. Today, when authority changes the teaching of the Church on the definitive revelation of God in Christ, on marriage, on Holy Communion, on the death penalty, on the 'blessability' of same-sex unions, etc., it is hard to say that using a fuller, older breviary can be considered grave matter, let alone mortal sin. Trads often lack ecclesial, historical and theological perspective, alas. Following rules — even stupid ones — is often easier than thinking."

EXPERT OPINION #3: DIOCESAN PRIEST AND CANON LAWYER

"At first glance, it would seem that the command to pray the office must be fulfilled by the use of an edition that has been promulgated and proposed for its fulfilment. From this perspective, only the Paul VI office or the John XXIII office would fulfil the obligation, especially from the vantage of 'public prayer of the Church,' i.e., not something done out of personal devotion.[2]

"However, while it is true that the legislation (in *Summorum Pontificum* Art. 9 n. 3) only specifically mentions the 1962, I still think there is room for the pre-conciliar breviary. Two aspects argue in favor of this: antinomy and *lacuna legis*.

"Some would argue that this matter falls into an issue of antinomy—two laws or norms belonging to the same juridical ordering, which take place in the same space and attribute incompatible legal consequences to a certain factual situation, which prevents their simultaneous application; in other words, a factual situation with two or more legal consequences that are incompatible because of two rules. So, one might look for a 'legislative silence' that would speak in favor of the freedom to use an older breviary. Silence is of far greater canonical value than most people realize.

"Moreover, a failure to specifically *proscribe* the recitation of the pre-55 breviary would lend support to its use based on the well-established canonical practice of respecting custom; indeed, the elucidation of this issue should be based on analogous situations, e.g., what happens with the missal. Even in this iconoclastic period

---

[2] A clause in *Rubricarum Instructum* of Pope John XXIII seems intended to close the lid on the issue (mind you, only for those with an obligation to the Divine Office): no. 3, "Item statuta, privilegia, indulta et consuetudines cuiuscumque generis, etiam saecularia et immemorabilia, immo specialissima atque individua mentione digna, quae his rubricis obstant, revocantur." ("Likewise, statutes, privileges, indults, and customs of any kind whatsoever—even secular and immemorial ones, indeed those most special and worthy of individual mention—which are contrary to these rubrics, are revoked.") However, the pope left an exclusion clause in no. 3: *quae his rubricis obstant* ("which are contrary to these rubrics"). What exactly this amounts to would need further investigation. Of considerable interest in this connection is the claim of Abbé Didier Bonneterre: "All canonists agree that the decrees of 1955 and 1960, which modified the Roman Breviary, did not abrogate the previous legislation. Thus, all those who use the Roman Breviary, whether according to the typical edition of 1914, or according to those of 1955 or 1960, fulfill the obligation of the Breviary" (*Le Bréviaire Romain*, Association Les Amis du Bréviaire Romain, Tours, 1979, p. ii).

we are living in, the Church has allowed the use of pre-62 ceremonies, and even though there is no *obligation* to celebrate Holy
Mass, nevertheless, one could say that the (at times) explicit and
(at other times) implicit approval of pre-62 ceremonies suggests
that the breviary could also fall into this approval, even with
silence on the subject.

"I would also argue that odious and dishonest things are not
to be presumed in law, and since the prayer of an older, at one
time normative breviary is certainly not odious, and the use of
it in no way bespeaks a desire to contravene the *mens legislatoris*,
one could in good conscience pray the pre-55 breviary.

"Furthermore, I would add that in the modern legislation for
the preconciliar liturgy — *Summorum Pontificum*, *Traditionis Custodes*, etc. — there is no explicit prohibition of the use of the
earlier breviaries, and one could argue that this falls into the
well-established legal principle of *odiosa sunt restringenda, favores
sunt amplianda*: odious laws — in other words, those that restrict
a right or freedom — must be interpreted strictly, in favor of
those who are subject to them; while favorable laws must be
interpreted broadly.

"Finally, we should take into consideration the actual state of
affairs in the mess of the postconciliar world. After Vatican II,
monastic communities were allowed to experiment and make up
their own divine office. You can find this out by visiting almost
any community at random: they are all doing different things.
There is a principle in the Church: 'office for office.' I was visiting
an abbey in another country and I noticed that their monastic
office was different. I wondered aloud to the prior if praying it
would suffice to fulfill my obligation, and he said: 'office for
office,' meaning, I could substitute the office prayed in common
in the abbey for the office I would have prayed from the breviary
(so, their morning prayer for my morning prayer, etc.). I do not
know how far this notion of 'office for office' could be taken,
but it seems to suggest that the Church regards it as sufficient if
a priest or religious offers the daily round of prayers and praises
in any accepted (or even tolerated) form."

EXPERT OPINION #4: ANOTHER BENEDICTINE MONK

"I was not convinced by the Benedictine's first opinion. When
he calls the priest's opinion 'legal positivism,' is he denying that

this is a matter of positive law? Or is he saying that *even though* it
is a matter of positive law, it should be obvious that this particular
law (requiring the Pius X office or the '62 office) is beyond the
authority of the legislator?

"As far as I can see, the only real argument he gives (in his first
response) is that the old office is much longer than that of Paul VI.
To me, this is not convincing. If I am bound by a lawful superior
to go to Texas, I don't fulfil my duty by going to China on the
grounds that it is a harder trip. The comparison is not simply
'more' in the sense that option 2 includes everything option 1
includes, plus some. That would be different. For the question is
not, can a priest pray the whole Paul VI office and *then* pray the
pre-55 in addition, but rather, can he replace the one with the
other? If the Church is a visible body with a visible head who has
a real legislative authority, one must allow that positive laws can
exist and should be obeyed, even when they are bad laws (I don't
mean sinful, but just mistaken or dumb, or otherwise flawed).

"The monk's second reply (to your implied objection from Pius
X) is more to the point. As far as I can see, the moral certainty
that we can stick to the old stuff arises predominantly from the
evidence that the new stuff is not simply 'less,' nor that it 'merely'
does away with a 1,000-year-old tradition, but that it is really
somehow against the Faith. I don't mean that the breviary itself
of Paul VI contains heresies. Rather, I think one can look at the
whole shebang since Vatican II, look at the current pontificate,
and reasonably conclude that there is an evil and anti-Catholic
trend which encompasses, more or less clearly, *all* the reforms
in the past several decades. The result would be a strong doubt
about the obligation to comply, and at least a reasonable guess that
sticking to pre-reform prayer is safe, despite what the pope says.

"I don't want to downplay the importance of tradition, but the
fact stands that there is no *clear* teaching (as far as I know) about
the limits of papal authority. For instance, we have no council that
says 'if anyone says a pope can change a tricentennial liturgical
custom, let him be anathema.' And, in fact, the texts we do have
tend in the opposite direction.

"As far as I can see, there is no way to know with certainty
that Pius X overstepped his authority and that his decree was
null. And, as a side note, I am not convinced that this is a purely
post-Vatican I problem either. Gregory VII tried aggressively to

replace the Mozarabic liturgy with the Roman Liturgy, invoking his papal right to do so. At the same time, I think there is a good deal of evidence to reasonably conclude—notice, I do not say conclude with certainty—that the traditions prior to Vatican II can be safely used, based on the overwhelming evidence that the Church has tended in an anti-Catholic direction since that time.

"The diocesan canonist's opinion is more convincing to me as well, but for different reasons. It acknowledges that this is a matter of positive law but seeks to answer the question within the framework of positive law. I am not qualified to assess the argument canonically but it seems reasonable. As the aforementioned moral argument is sufficient (in my mind at least), I don't really bother with trying to find solutions within the letter of the law."

MY RESPONSE TO THE LAST—AND IN GENERAL

I think the logically possible approaches are well summarized in the expert opinions 1, 2, and 3.

Does a pope have authority to require a certain form of prayer? I think the question is ambiguous. If the form he requires represents a radical break with the form required for centuries and centuries, then we might have a problem on our hands—one that could result in a true crisis of conscience. This is where the fateful combination of legal positivism and ever-expanding ultramontanism comes into the picture, for the question is rendered easy if you say the pope has absolute authority over everything liturgical (except for a highly distilled "form and matter" of sacraments), and that the only duty of the subordinate to obey his will (or his whims).

But since this is not the way the Church has behaved throughout her history—in fact, it is the opposite of the way she has behaved—and there are sound theological, anthropological, and moral reasons to think that this cannot be right, one may arrive at the position of the Benedictine monk who says it is absurd to believe that praying a traditional "received and approved" form of the liturgy could be wrong, or ruled out as sinful.

The Texas/China analogy fails because, in fact, we are talking about different forms or versions of the same thing, namely, the divine office by which the hours of the day are to be sanctified through the recitation of psalms and prayers. A form that is both *more ancient* and *more extensive* would satisfy a requirement that one must do something of the same kind that is *more recent* and *more restricted*. The only way it could be maintained that a later form *must* replace an earlier form is if there was something wrong with the earlier form.

Indeed, this is why, when Urban VIII changed the Latin of the breviary hymns, the religious communities (Benedictines, Cistercians, Dominicans, some others too) simply begged off and said they were content with the language of the hymns as they existed in their own offices. The new language and the old could exist side-by-side. Nor did that pope, or any other, dare to force the matter. That's because there once was respect for autonomy and diversity, as opposed to now, when everyone talks about these things but no one actually respects them.

The fact that there is no explicit statement that the pope cannot cancel out "received and approved rites" of venerable standing is because it would have seemed ridiculous to our forebears to think that he *could*. You might remember the episode at Vatican I:

> Now before the final vote on *Pastor Aeternus* at Vatican I, several Council Fathers were concerned that they would be voting for a doctrine that would give the pope absolute and unqualified jurisdictional authority. Various (documented) discussions were given by members of the Deputation of the Faith assuring the Council Fathers that this was not a correct understanding of the doctrine. That is, they (the Relators of the Deputation) stated that the pope, in his jurisdictional authority, does not have absolute and unqualified jurisdictional authority. One Council Father, however, an American named Bishop [Augustin] Vérot of Savannah, apparently was not convinced, and requested that specific qualifying statements (to the effect that the pope's jurisdictional authority is qualified) be inserted into the texts of the schemas. He was told that the Council Fathers had not come to Rome "to hear buffooneries." In other words, if this bishop had understood the theological context of the schema, he would not have put himself in such an embarrassing situation.[3]

I rather regret that it seemed so obvious to the fathers of Vatican I, because I think the qualifying language that Bishop Vérot

---

[3] Brill, *The Great Sacred Music Reform*, 47n25.

wanted would have been exceedingly useful at present. Of course, when the German bishops got around to explaining Vatican I to Prussia,[4] they did add a number of valuable clarifications, though again, their document suffers from vagueness. Just what does "human arbitrariness" amount to? What does it look like? How do we know it when we see it? Assuredly, it seems that *today* we know it when we see it, because popes have gone so far off the deep end in this or that instance.[5]

Now, if it could be shown that anything demanded by a pope was contrary to the Faith or to sound morals, that in itself would be a reason to say no to it and to stick with what was there before. This, evidently, is what we must do with something like *Amoris Laetitia*. But it seems also true to say that if something demanded by a pope is followed by a period of uninterrupted institutional chaos or decline, it becomes suspect by that very fact; or (perhaps this is to say the same thing) that in a period of institutional chaos or decline, it is legitimate to maintain the "status quo ante," much as Lefebvre maintained that he realized he had to stick with the missal prior to the deformations of the 1960s that led to the *Novus Ordo* of 1969. (Sadly, neither he nor the Society has ever quite figured out that the changes in the 1950s were part of the same process of deformation and therefore should have been rejected for exactly the same reason. It was the same people with the same principles who were behind both phases, before and after the Council.)

At this time in particular, when the postconciliar autodemolition of the Church is plain for all to see, there is no reason to doubt anymore that the liturgical revolution — which had its ill-starred conception in Pius X's hyperpapalist revamp of the breviary, its ominous childhood in Pius XII's rewriting of Holy Week, and its monstrous adulthood in the ruptures of Paul VI — is something that cannot be of God, cannot be truly "of the Church," and cannot be for the good of souls.

---

[4] Kwasniewski, "Objections and Replies on *Pastor Aeternus*," in idem, *Bound by Truth*, 30–38.
[5] I tried to bring some clarity to this topic in my lecture "The Pope's Boundedness to Tradition as a Legislative Limit: Replying to Ultramontanist Apologetics." Fr. Réginald-Marie Rivoire also discusses this point in his tract *Does "Traditionis Custodes" Pass the Juridical Rationality Test?* (to which the answer is, no).

Granted, each stage is worse than the one before, such that, as I argue in chapter 12 of *Once and Future Roman Rite*, there are *fewer* objections one can make to earlier stages and *more* to later ones, which also implies that adhering to the earlier is less problematic than adhering to the later (e.g., praying the breviary of Pius X is not as bad as using the Holy Week of Pius XII, and using the Holy Week of Pius XII is not as bad as using the missal of Paul VI). But since there is a real continuity of principles, one is fully justified in taking the whole series as a single process, and saying, as a matter of coherent traditionalism: *I will pray the breviary and the missal as they existed prior to this revolutionary process.*

Benedictines are fortunate in this regard, as they have the unchanged *cursus psalmorum* of St. Benedict, nice editions of their choir books, and an altar missal from the first half of the twentieth century. All this is "ready to go" in a way that makes the Roman situation look terribly messy by comparison. That's why I'm not surprised that a number of secular clergy have become or seek to become Benedictine oblates: it gives them a direct channel to a full set of traditional liturgical books still in use in a fair number of abbeys in communion with the Holy See.

APPENDIX 2

Outline of Changes to the Roman Missal and Breviary Between 1955 and 1962[1]

PAUL CAVENDISH

PREFATORY NOTE BY PETER KWASNIEWSKI

In the slow but steady work of restoring the Roman liturgical tradition, it seems that we are never quite fully equipped with all the resources we might wish to have at any given moment. There is work being done today, for instance, that would have been mightily helpful to have decades ago. At the moment there is a burning need for reprints of the pre-55 breviary (both Roman and Monastic) and of the pre-55 altar missal. But things get done when they get done. An example of just such a precious boon is the following pair of detailed comparative charts, prepared by expert calendarist and rubrician Paul Cavendish of St. Lawrence Press fame.

The idea that the post-conciliar changes to the Roman rite (whose solid outline certainly was already in place in the early 1950s, as we shall see in a moment) just came out of thin air and were all the fault of Vatican II, or Paul VI, or both, is simply impossible to sustain from a closer look of the patterns indicated on Cavendish's charts. Appendix A of H. A. Reinhold's 1960 book *Bringing the Mass to the People* contains a summary of the proposals emerging from Maria Laach (1951), Ste Odile (1952), and Lugano (1953). They read as a veritable blueprint for the *Novus Ordo*:

> A resume of the liturgical resolutions of the liturgical congresses at Maria Laach (1951), Ste Odile (1952) and Lugano (1953).

---

[1] Published as "An Essential Resource for Restorationists: Detailed Charts Comparing Pre-'55, '55, and '62 Mass and Office," *New Liturgical Movement*, July 6, 2022.

This resume is taken from the official report on the Third Liturgical Congress, held from September 15 to 18 in 1953, that was prepared by Luigi Agustoni and Johannes Wagner (published at Lugano by the Centro di Liturgia Pastorale) which sums up the two preceding congresses, incorporating the main resolutions taken at these meetings.

The first seventeen of these proposals had already been mentioned at the Maria Laach meeting two years previously.

1. Abolition of the present duplication of readings.

2. Omission of the Judica, etc.

3. The second part of the Mass[2] should be called: the Liturgy of the Word. It should be carried out *in choro*, not at the altar.

4. Never more than *one* Collect (with rare exceptions).

5. A three- or four-year *cycle of Lessons* and *Gospels* for Sundays.

6. Less frequent recitation of the Credo.

7. The *Prex fidelium* (Bidding Prayers) should be reintroduced as the conclusion of the Liturgy of the Word. Omit the Dominus vobiscum at the beginning of the Offertory.

8. The sacred vessels should not be on the altar before the Offertory.

9. More Prefaces, but only those which refer to the *Memoria Passionis*.

10. The priest should wait for the end of the Sanctus to continue the Mass. The different Amens during the Canon should be eliminated.

11. No Confiteor, etc., at Communion time.

12. No Last Gospel. The Last Blessing ends the Mass.

13. Rename the *Secreta*: "Oratio super oblata", and make it the audible conclusion of the Offertory.

14. Sing the Great Doxology at the end of the Canon; eliminate its five signs of the cross and elevate the two Sacred Species during the Doxology. No genuflection before this elevation and perhaps no genuflection at all.

---

[2] The "first part" would be everything prior to the readings, from the confession of sins through the Collect.

15. After the Pater noster: regroup the prayers and ceremonies and find a way to have the congregation participate in the Pax.

16. Develop the interval between Communion and Post-communion (prayers and singing, consult other liturgies).

17. Regulate the use of Ite, missa est and Benedicamus Domino (see the new regulation on Holy Thursday).

Proposals 18–26 had already been mentioned at the Conference at Ste Odile.

18. The revised Easter Vigil is the model of the principles which should govern future reforms.

19. Sing or recite aloud the Per ipsum (Great Doxology); no signs of the cross; elevate the two Species until the Amen of the people; no genuflection here, or only after the Amen [repeating no. 14].

20. No Amen after the Pater noster; sing or recite aloud the Libera nos; no sign of the cross with the empty paten, no kiss [anticipating projects at Lugano].

21. Place the first Domine Jesu Christe immediately after the Libera (or suppress it entirely); follow the Pax Domini sit semper vobiscum with no ceremony of the Host; no response of the people; give Pax afterward (this is spelled out in detail on pp. 242–3 of the report).

22. Breaking of the Host takes place after the Pax, with no accompanying ceremony, while the congregation sings the Agnus Dei; at low Mass the priest says it after the Fractio. The two Communion prayers should then follow or be suppressed (see pp. 242–4 of the report).

23. The celebrant receives half the Host, the other half is either given to those who serve at the altar or distributed with the ciborium.

24. No Confiteor, etc., at Communion time; shortening of the "Corpus" prayer during the distribution (p. 239 of the report elaborates the 1951 Maria Laach resolution).

25. Have the Communio sung solemnly during the distribution, even in the vernacular.

26. At the end of the Mass: Ite missa est (only), Deo gratias, kiss of the altar (no Placeat), blessing, and people's Amen. No Last Gospel or Leonine prayers.

These resolutions were proposed to the Sacred Congregation of Rites, and are the basis of most of the suggestions
made in this book. We ask the readers to keep in mind,
especially when this book seems to be bold or radical,
that the company we are keeping consists of the cream
of liturgical scholars.

In 1957, eminent liturgical historian Archdale King summarized
the Lugano plan as follows:

> A revision of the solemn Mass, little short of revolution-
> ary, was discussed at an international liturgical congress
> held at Lugano in September 1953, with the intention
> of simplifying the rite, removing what is redundant or
> superfluous, and giving the faithful a more active part in
> the liturgy. There is, however, no certitude that Rome will
> accede to all these changes, and in any case her innate
> conservatism and caution would preclude any immediate
> acceptance. A revision of the Roman missal and breviary
> is certainly under consideration, but what will be done,
> and when it will be finished, it is impossible to say.[3]

Cum nostra hac aetate and *Maxima redemptionis nostrae mysteria*,
both of 1955, were of course the tipping point, though the 1951
and 1952 "Easter Vigil" permissions presaged something big. There
was lesser tinkering too, such as the *editio VI post typicam* of the
Missal in 1953 which anticipated some of the 1962MR changes,
such as short conclusions. Incidentally, Bugnini wrote a very
useful article in *Ephemerides Liturgicae* about that...

In any case, the charts should be fairly self-explanatory, and
will repay close study.

---

[3] Archdale A. King, *Liturgy of the Roman Church* (Bruce Publishing Co.,
1957), 45.

OUTLINE OF CHANGES TO
THE ROMAN MISSAL BETWEEN 1955 AND 1962

		PRE-1956	1956	1962
GENERAL		Body of Missal prefaced by Pius V's *Quo primum* etc., *De Anno et ejus Partibus*, Calendar, then *Rubricae Generales Missalis* (20 sections), *Additiones et Variationes*,[1] *Ritus Servandus*, *De Defectibus*, Prayers of Preparation and Thanksgiving, and diagrams of how to cense the *oblata* and altar.		Motu proprio *Rubricarum instructum*[2] inserted after *Quo primum* etc., new *Rubricae Generales*, *Rubricae Generales Missalis Romani* replacing the previous version, *Additiones et Variationes* removed (as a consequence of the new General Rubrics), new *Ritus Servandus* (replacing previous text), new *De Defectibus* & new image of how to cense free-standing altar added.[3]
		Entrance, offertory and communion chants appear as *Introitus*, *Offertorium* & *Communio*.	In Holy Week[4] renamed *Antiphona ad Introitum*, *Antiphona ad Offertorium* & *Antiphona ad Communionem*.	Terminology extended to the entire Liturgical Year.
CLASSIFICATION OF LITURGICAL DAYS		Ancient system of days of nine lessons (at Mattins) or three lessons, further classified into Doubles (four sub-groups), Semi-doubles, and Simples.	Semi-doubles abolished[5]; semi-double feasts become simples; semi-double Sundays become doubles.	All days re-classified into I Class, II Class, III Class & IV Class.

	PRE-1956	1956	1962
CALENDAR	Vigils: 3 privileged Vigils; 14 Common Vigils in the Universal Calendar	1 Privileged Vigil abolished; 9 Common Vigils abolished[6]	Series of feasts abolished from the Calendar: St. Peter's Chair in Rome (Jan 18), Finding of the Holy Cross (May 3), St. John Before the Latin Gate (May 6), Apparition of St. Michael (May 8), St. Leo II (Jul 3), St. Anacletus (Jul 13), St. Peter in Chains (Aug 1), Finding of St. Stephen (Aug 3), Commem. of St. Vitalis (Apr 28).[8]
	Three classes of Octave: Privileged (three subgroups), Common and Simple (minimum of 23 Octaves in Diocesan Calendars)	Octaves abolished except for Nativity of the Lord, Easter & Pentecost[7]	
		Solemnity of St. Joseph (Third Wednesday after Easter) and its Octave abolished, replaced by St. Joseph the Worker (May 1). Title of "Patron of Universal Church" transferred to March 19 feast.	
		(1962) Feasts transferred: St. Irenaeus (Jun 28 to Jul 3); St. John Mary Vianney (Aug 9 to Aug 8), both to allow full celebration of Vigils on original days.	
		(1962) Feasts reduced to commemoration[9]: St. George (Apr 23), Our Lady of Mt. Carmel (Jul 16), St. Alexius (Jul 17), SS Cyriacus, Largus & Smaragdus (Aug 8), Impression of Stigmata of St. Francis (Sep 17), SS Eustace and Companions (Sep 20), Our Lady of Ransom (Sep 24), St. Thomas of Canterbury (Dec 29), St. Sylvester (Dec 31), Seven Sorrows of Our Lady in Passiontide.	

		(1962)
CALENDAR		(1962) Feasts' names changed: Circumcision (Jan 1)[10] to Octave of the Nativity, Most Holy Rosary (Oct 7) to BVM of the Rosary.
CHOICE OF MASS	During Lent, Passiontide & Ember Days when a double (not of the I or II class) or semi-double feast occurs (e.g. St. Gregory the Great), the celebrant of a private[11] Mass may say either the Mass of the feast, with commemoration of the feria etc., or Mass of the feria with commemoration of the feast.[12] The same choice when a feast and vigil occur.	(1962) In the Temporal series of Masses new seasonal headings inserted: *Tempus Adventus, Tempus Nativitatis, Tempus Epiphaniae, Tempus per Annum ante Septuagesimal, Tempus Septuagesimae, Tempus Quadragesimae, Tempus Passionis, Hebdomada Sancta, Tempus Paschatis, Tempus Acensionis & Tempus per Annum post Pentecosten.* Days of Advent, Lent & Ember Days raised to II Class, taking precedence over III class feasts. Mass must be said of the feria.[13]
GESTURES & VOICE	Celebrant uses three degrees of vocalisation: clear, secret, and mid-voice.[14] Four types of bow used at Mass: 2 of the body, deep and moderate; 2 of the head, deep and slight. When at the corners of the altar, Celebrant bows to the altar cross when saying *Gloria Patri* (e.g. at Introit), the Holy Name, etc. During Penitential Masses (e.g. weekdays of Advent, Lent, Ember Days & Masses for the Dead) choir and servers kneel for collects and post-communion, and from the *Sanctus* until the response to *Pax Domini* has been sung.	Two degrees of voice only; mid-voice abolished. Bows simplified to bow of the body and bow of the head. When not at the centre the Celebrant bows to the book, not to the altar cross. At Penitential Masses & Masses for the Dead, kneeling period reduced to from the *Sanctus* until before the *Pater noster.*

	PRE-1956	1956	1962
VESTURE	At Solemn Mass deacon and subdeacon wear violet folded chasubles *planetis plicatis* during penitential seasons of Advent, Lent & Holy Week, the September Ember Days and for the blessing of Candles on Feb 2 and at the beginning of the Vigil of Pentecost. Black *planetis placatis* on Good Friday.	Folded chasubles abolished during Holy Week. (Pentecost Vigil preceremonies abolished.)	Folded chasubles abolished altogether. Blessing of Candles on Feb 2 carried out in white vestments.
BLESSING OF LUSTRAL WATER	Collects *Immensam, Deus, qui, ad salutem & Deus, invictae* have long conclusions (*Per Dominum nostrum Jesum Christum* etc.).		Collects have short conclusion (*Per Christum Dominum nostrum*).[15]
PRAYERS AT THE FOOT OF THE ALTAR	*Introibo ad altare Dei & Judica me Deus* (Ps. 42) and confession of Celebrant and ministers said in all Masses except those of Passiontide and Masses for the Dead (in those cases the Psalm, only, is omitted).	Omitted entirely Palm Sunday and Easter Vigil.	Omitted entirely on Palm Sunday, Easter Vigil, Candlemas, Ash Wednesday, the four Rogation Days, and certain other Masses according the new rubrics of the Roman Pontifical.

COLLECTS	Occurring Offices commemorated[16] on all but the greatest feasts. E.g. on Sunday within the Octave of the Sacred Heart (Pentecost III), 30 Jun 2019, the following Offices were commemorated: (i) St. Paul the Apostle, (ii) St. Peter the Apostle, (iii) Octave of the Sacred Heart & (iv) Octave of the Nativity of St. John the Baptist, making five collects etc. at Mass.	Occurring saints' feasts still commemorated on Sundays.	Commemorations of most saints not made on Sundays, II class feasts commemorated at said Masses only.
	On days below the rank of double, additional collects "of the Season" said in addition to occurring Offices. E.g. in Advent, from the first Sunday, the Missal prescribes the addition of a second collect of the BVM, *Deus, qui de beatae* and a third collect for either the Church, *Ecclesiae*, or for the Pope, *Deus, omnium*.[17] Normally, but not always, three collects on Sundays and days of semi-double rank and lower.	Prayers of the Season abolished.	
	In low Masses on simple days, celebrant may add votive collects in addition to those prescribed by the rubrics so that the total number of collects is five or seven.	Number of additional collects reduced to two.	Theoretical maximum of two additional collects—but this would be very rare: one votive collect allowed on IV class days. Increased occasions where a prayer is added "under one conclusion" to the prayers of the day, e.g. Mission Sunday.
FLECT-AMUS GENUA	*Flectamus genua* chanted by the deacon, *Levate* by the Sub-deacon (or said by the server).	During Holy Week *Levate* chanted by the deacon (or said by Celebrant).	New rule extended throughout Liturgical Year.

	PRE-1956	1956	1962
PERICOPES	Celebrant reads all texts in the Missal at the altar including pericopes.	Celebrant does not read pericopes during new Holy Week but does so during the rest of the year.	Celebrant does not read pericopes (but does read Gradual, etc.).
	Celebrant censed after Gospel at sung Mass without ministers.		Celebrant not censed at sung Mass without ministers.
	Ember Days with additional lessons must all be read by celebrant and may not be omitted.		Short form of Ember Saturday Masses permitted with one OT reading, Epistle and Gospel.
CREED	Recited on Sundays and higher-ranking feasts and their Octaves, on feasts of Angels, Doctors, St Mary Magdalen, etc.	Creed restricted to Sundays, Double I Class feasts, feasts of Our Lord & Our Lady, principal feasts of Apostles, Doctors & Solemn Votive Masses.	Creed no longer said on feasts of Doctors or Solemn Votive Masses (sung only in Votive Masses of I Class).
COMMUNION	Rubrics[18] directed that a *Sanctus* candle be lit from after the *Sanctus* until the end of Communion. (Torches at Pontifical Mass, and by custom Solemn Mass, fulfilled the same function.)		Rubrics say that where the custom of the *Sanctus* candle prevails it should be preserved, implying that it is not to be followed otherwise; torches at solemn Mass in *RS* (new) *VIII*, 8.
	Deacon at Pontifical Mass, and by custom at Solemn Mass, sings *Confiteor* before Communion, *Misereatur* and *Indulgentiam* said by Celebrant. At Masses without sacred ministers, MC or server recites Confiteor.	*Confiteor* etc. suppressed on Maundy Thursday.	*Confiteor* etc. suppressed throughout the Liturgical Year[19] except during the "Solemn Afternoon Liturgical Action" on Good Friday.

COMMUNION	Where Communion is to be given from Hosts reserved in the tabernacle, Celebrant genuflects before removing ciborium from the tabernacle and then genuflects again after uncovering the ciborium.[20]		Celebrant genuflects once only, after opening tabernacle.
	Ablution cup[21] containing wine and water offered to Communicants after they have received by a server with a purificator (this rite was, sadly, often omitted).		Text suppressed in new *RS*.
DIS-MISSAL	*Ite, missa est* said when the Mass contains the *Gloria in excelsis*, otherwise *Benedicamus Domino*. (In Masses of the Dead, *Requiescant in pace*.)	Maundy Thursday Mass modified to have *Benedicamus Domino* as the dismissal.	All Masses have *Ite, missa est*, including those in violet vestments. *Benedicamus Domino* only said when a procession or other function follows.
LAST GOSPEL	Last Gospel never omitted. Proper last Gospel when a commemoration has its own proper Gospel, e.g. Lenten Week days, Apostles, etc.	Last Gospel omitted on Palm Sunday, Maundy Thursday & Holy Saturday.	Last Gospel omitted on Palm Sunday, Maundy Thursday, Holy Saturday, Rogation Days, *Corpus Christi* etc. whenever a procession or function follows Mass.
	Only two proper last Gospels: third Mass of Christmas and Palm Sunday when Palms not blessed.		Only one proper last Gospel, Palm Sunday when Palms not blessed.

OUTLINE OF CHANGES TO
THE ROMAN BREVIARY BETWEEN 1955 AND 1962

	PRE-1956	1956	1962
GENERAL	Breviary prefaced by Pius V's *Quod a nobis* etc., *De Anno et ejus Partibus*, Calendar, then *Rubricae Generales Breviarii* (37 chapters), *Additiones et Variationes*,[1] Tables of occurrence and concurrence, then the Ordinary of the Office, the Hours of each day of the week, the *Temporale*, and the *Sanctorale*.		Breviary prefaced by printer's decree, after *Quod a nobis* etc. Motu proprio *Rubricarum instructum*, new *Rubricae Generales*, *Rubricae Generales Breviarii Romani*, (replacing old General Rubrics and *Additiones et Variationes*) inserted, Calendar, *Temporale* (with seasonal sub-headings *Tempus Adventus* etc. as in the Missal), the Hours for each day of the week, then the *Sanctorale*.
	Usually arranged in four volumes: *Hiemalis* (Advent to the Saturday before Lent), *Verna* (Lent to Ember Saturday in Pentecost), *Aestiva* (Trinity Sunday to Saturday of the last week of August[2]) and *Autumnalis* (first Sunday of September to the Saturday before Advent).		Usually arranged in two volumes *Pars Prior / Tomus Prior* (Advent to Ember Saturday in Pentecost) and *Pars Altera / Tomus Alter* (Trinity Sunday to Saturday before Advent).
			In private recitation of the Office *Dominus vobiscum* no longer said but *Domine, exaudi orationem meam.*
			Some Psalms & Canticles have verses omitted: at Saturday Lauds II *Audite, caeli* is reduced from 65 to 37 verses; on the Nativity of the Lord, during the Octave and on the feast of Christ the King Ps. 88 is reduced from 51 to 36 verses; on the feast of the Transfiguration Ps. 88 is reduced to 17 verses.

CLASSIFICATION OF LITURGICAL DAYS	Ancient system of days of nine lessons (at Mattins) or three lessons, further classified into Doubles (I Class, II Class, Greater-doubles & doubles), Semi-doubles and Simples.	Semi-double rank abolished[3]; semi-double feasts become simples; Semi-double Sundays become doubles.	All days re-classified into I Class, II Class, III Class (most former doubles) & IV Class (most former simples).
	Office of Double and Semi-double feasts extends from first Vespers (on the eve) through to second Vespers and Compline. Office of Simple feasts extends from Vespers on the eve through to None. Office of Vigils extends from Mattins to None.	First Vespers limited[4] to Sundays, Doubles of the I Class & II Class (and certain Greater-doubles when occurring on a Sunday).[5]	First Vespers limited to Sundays and I Class feasts (and certain other days when they take the place of a Sunday).[6]
CALENDAR	Vigils: 3 Privileged Vigils; 14 Common Vigils in the Universal Calendar	1 Privileged Vigil abolished; 9 Common Vigils abolished[7]	Vigils become II Class.
	Three classes of Octave: Privileged (three sub-groups), Common, and Simple (mimimum of 23 Octaves in Diocesan Calendars)	Octaves abolished except for Nativity of the Lord, Easter & Pentecost.[8] Days within Octaves become doubles (although no change to Nativity Octave).	Days within Octaves of Easter and Pentecost become I Class; within Nativity Octave II Class.
	Sundays: Advent I, Lent I, II, III, IV, Passion & Palm Sundays were Semi-doubles of I Class. Low Sunday Great-double I Class.	Sundays of Advent, Lent up to Low Sunday all become D1Cl with priority in both occurrence and concurrence.[9]	Sundays of Advent, Lent, Passiontide, and Low Sunday become I Class Sundays.
	Septuagesima, Sexagesima, Quinquagesima, Advent II, III, IV Semi-doubles of the II Class.	Sundays of Advent II, III, & IV raised to I Class.	
	"Green Sundays" all Semi-double rank.	Green Sundays become doubles (but antiphons not doubled).	The 'Gesima and Green Sundays become II Class Sundays (antiphons doubled).

	PRE-1956	1956	1962
CALENDAR	Anticipated and resumed Sundays: Depending on the year a Sunday after the Epiphany, or after Pentecost, was anticipated before Septuagesima or Advent. When a major feast was celebrated on a Sunday, the Sunday Mass was resumed during the week with certain privileges.	Sundays never anticipated or resumed.	
		Solemnity of St. Joseph (Third Wednesday after Easter) and its Octave abolished, replaced by St. Joseph the Worker (May 1). Title of "Patron of Universal Church" transferred to March 19 feast.	Series of feasts abolished from the Calendar: St. Peter's Chair in Rome (Jan 18), Finding of the Holy Cross (May 3), St. John Before the Latin Gate (May 6), Apparition of St. Michael (May 8), St. Leo II (Jul 3), St. Anacletus (Jul 13), St. Peter in Chains (Aug 1), Finding of St. Stephen (Aug 3), Commem. of St. Vitalis (Apr 28).
		(1962) Feasts transferred: St. Irenaeus (Jun 28 to Jul 3); St. John Mary Vianney (Aug 9 to Aug 8) both to allow full celebration of Vigils on original days.	
		(1962) Feasts reduced to commemoration[10]: St. George (Apr 23), Our Lady of Mt. Carmel (Jul 16), St. Alexius (Jul 17), SS Cyriacus, Largus & Smaragdus (Aug 8), Impression of Stigmata of St. Francis (Sep 17), SS Eustace and Companions (Sep 20), Our Lady of Ransom (Sep 24), St. Thomas of Canterbury (Dec 29), St. Sylvester (Dec 31), Seven Sorrows of Our Lady in Passiontide.	
		(1962) Feasts' names changed: Circumcision (Jan 1)[11] to Octave of the Nativity, Most Holy Rosary (Oct 7) to BVM of the Rosary.	
	All Sundays (except those of Easter and Pentecost), doubles and semi-doubles have Martins of three nocturns each with three lessons (except days within the Octaves of Easter and Pentecost). Simple feast and ferial days have a single nocturn of three lessons.	All Sundays reduced Martins of a single nocturn of three lessons.[12] Only I Class and II Class feasts have three nocturns, all other days have a single nocturn of three lessons.	

MATTINS	Aperi, Domine said kneeling before all Offices, or groups of Hours.	Suppressed.	
	Pater, Ave & Credo said sub silentio before Domine, labia mea aperies.	Silent prayers abolished. Mattins begins with Domine, labia mea aperies.	
	Antiphons said in full (doubled) on double feasts; on semi-doubles and below, only the first fragment before the asterisk is said before psalm(s).	(On Green Sundays although now double, antiphons not doubled.)	All antiphons doubled at all Hours regardless of rank of feast.
	Psalms: On D1Cl, D2Cl, psalms proper to the feast or common; proper psalms on some other doubles; on ferial days psalms as appointed for the weekday.		
	1st nocturn lessons transferred on some days, e.g. anticipated before Septuagesima and Advent, or resumed, e.g. when a greater feast is celebrated on some "green" Sundays, the Sunday lessons are said on a following week day.	Lessons never transferred, always of occurring scripture or the common.	
	On some days the ninth lesson is of a commemorated Office or Sunday, e.g. 9th lesson of 'green' Sunday when an Apostle's feast falls on a Sunday.	Commemoration of another Office at Mattins by a 9th lesson abolished.	
	Mattins in choro always combined with Lauds except at the Nativity of the LORD when Midnight Mass interpolated between Mattins and Lauds.		Mattins can be separated from Lauds in all circumstances.
	In private recitation Mattins ends with Pater (sub silentio) after the verse Fidelium animae etc.	Silent Pater abolished.	

	PRE-1956	1956	1962
LAUDS	*Pater & Ave* said *sub silentio* before *Deus, in adjutorium.*	Silent prayers abolished. Lauds begin with *Deus, in adjutorium.*	
	Antiphons said in full (doubled) on double feasts, on semi-doubles and below, only the first fragment before the asterisk is said before psalm(s).	(On Green Sundays although now double, antiphons not doubled.)	All antiphons doubled at all Hours regardless of rank of feast.
	Psalms: On D1Cl, D2Cl, psalms proper to the feast or common; Sunday psalms on some other doubles, including those with proper antiphons, e.g. St. Agnes, otherwise psalms from the Psalter for the weekday as on ferial days.		
	Ferial *preces* sung, kneeling, on penitential days.	Ferial *preces* restricted to Wednesdays & Fridays of Lent, Passiontide & Advent, and Ember Days outside Pentecost.	
	Commemorations[13] of all occurring Offices on all but the greatest feasts.	Abolished (except a limited number[14]) on feasts and Sundays of 1Cl & privileged ferial days. One commemoration allowed on feasts and Sundays of 2Cl. Two commemorations allowed on other days.	Commemorations classified as "privileged" and "ordinary." On I Class days only one privileged commemoration allowed. On II Class Sundays one commemoration of a II Class feast allowed (omitted if a privileged commemoration has to be made). Other II Class days one privileged or one ordinary commemoration allowed. On III and IV Class days two commemorations allowed.

LAUDS	Suffrage of the Saints (three forms) sung on Semi-doubles (outside of Octaves) after last commemoration.	Suffrage of the Saints abolished.	
	Lauds end with *Pater* (*sub silentio*) after verse *Fidelium animae* etc. and immediately followed by Antiphon to the BVM *Salve Regina* etc. (When Office is said *in choro* the Antiphon is said when leaving choir after other Offices.)	Silent *Pater* abolished; Antiphon to BVM only after Compline.	
	Pater, Ave & Credo said *sub silentio* before *Deus, in adjutorium.*	Silent prayers abolished. Prime begins with *Deus, in adjutorium.*	
	Antiphons never doubled, even on greatest days.		All antiphons doubled at all Hours regardless of rank of feast.
PRIME	Psalms: On D1Cl, D2Cl & certain other days, festal psalms (Pss. 53, 118i & 118ii); on ferial days, psalms as appointed for the weekday.	Festal psalms only for D1Cl, all other feasts psalms of the weekday.	
	On penitential days when the second scheme of Lauds is used, the psalm displaced by the *Miserere* is added to Prime (e.g. on Mondays the first psalm of Lauds, Ps. 46 *Omnes gentes*). The psalmody of Prime becomes 23, 118i, 118ii & 46.		No fourth psalm added at Prime. On penitential Sundays where the fourth psalm had been added, Ps.53 added to 118i & 118ii (the festal arrangement in the Tridentine Office!).
	Chapter *Regi saeculorum* when the Office is festal, *Pacem et veritatem* on ferial days and Vigils.		Chapter always *Regi saeculorum*; *Pacem et veritatem* abolished.

	PRE-1956	1956	1962
PRIME	In responsory after the chapter, the versicle *Qui sedes* changes during some seasons or feasts, e.g. *Qui venturus es* in Advent, *Qui natus es* on feasts of the BVM, or when an occurring feast or Octave with a proper versicle is commemorated.	Commemorations no longer give Office of the day a changed versicle.	
	Dominical *preces* (a short series of intercessions in V & R format) said on Offices of Semi-doubles (outside of Octaves) and below.	Dominical *preces* abolished.[15]	
	Ferial *preces* (a longer series of intercessions including the Dominical *preces*) sung kneeling on penitential days.	Ferial *preces* abolished except at Lauds and Vespers on certain days.[16]	
	Short lesson taken from the feast, common, or season (it is the same as the chapter at None).		Short lesson always taken from the season, not from None.
	Prime ends with *Pater* (*sub silentio*) after *Dominus nos benedicat* & *Amen*.	Silent *Pater* abolished.	
TERCE, SEXT & NONE	Offices begin with *Pater* & *Ave sub silentio*.	Silent prayers abolished. Hours begin with *Deus, in adjutorium*.	
	Antiphons never doubled, even on greatest feasts.		All antiphons doubled at all Hours regardless of rank of feast.
	Psalms of Sunday at all D1Cl, D2Cl and certain other feasts; on ferial days from the psalter.	Sunday psalms only for D1Cl. Psalms for the weekday/Sunday all other days.	
	When ferial *preces* are sung at Lauds, short series of ferial *preces* sung, kneeling, at the Hours.	Ferial *preces* abolished at Minor Hours.	
	Offices end with *Pater* (*sub silentio*) after the verse *Fidelium animae* etc.	Silent *Pater* abolished.	

VESPERS	*Pater & Ave* said *sub silentio* before *Deus, in adjutorium.*	Silent prayers abolished. Vespers begin with *Deus, in adjutorium.*	All antiphons doubled at all Hours regardless of rank of feast.
	Antiphons said in full (doubled) on double feasts; on semi-doubles and below, only the first fragment before the asterisk is said before psalm(s).	(On Green Sundays although now double, antiphons not doubled.)	
	Psalms: On D1Cl, D2Cl, psalms proper to the feast or common; Sunday psalms on some other doubles, including those with proper antiphons, e.g., St. Agnes, otherwise psalms from the Psalter for the weekday as on ferial days.		
	Ferial *preces* sung, kneeling, on penitential days.	Ferial *preces* restricted to Wednesdays and Fridays of Lent, Passiontide & Advent, & Ember Wednesdays and Fridays outside Pentecost.	
	Commemorations of occurring Offices after collect of the day on all but greatest feasts.	Abolished (except a limited number[17]) on feasts and Sundays of 1Cl & privileged ferial days. One commemoration allowed on feasts and Sundays of 2Cl. Two commemorations allowed on other days.[18]	Only "privileged" commemorations allowed: Sundays, I Class feasts, days within Christmas Octave, Days of Advent, Lent, Passiontide & Ember Days.
	Suffrage of the Saints (three forms) sung on Semi-doubles (outside of Octaves) after last commemoration.	Suffrage abolished.	
	Vespers end with *Pater* (*sub silentio*) after verse *Fidelium animae* etc.	Silent *Pater* abolished.	

	PRE-1956	1956	1962
COMPLINE	Office begins with *Jube, domne*.		When said as final Hour of the day an examination of conscience may be inserted in place of the *Pater* before the *Confiteor*.
	Antiphon never doubled before psalms or canticle.		All antiphons doubled at all Hours regardless of rank of feast.
	Psalms of Sunday used for D1Cl, D2Cl and certain other feasts; on ferial days psalms from the Psalter.		
	Dominical *preces* sung on Semi-doubles (outside of Octaves) and below, when ferial *preces* sung at Vespers the Dominical *preces* at Compline are sung kneeling.	Dominical *preces* abolished.	
	Compline ends with Antiphon to the BVM etc. after blessing, followed by *Pater, Ave & Credo* (*sub silentio*).	Silent *Pater, Ave & Credo* abolished.	
	Sacrosanctae, Pater & Ave said, kneeling, at the end of the Office of the day	Suppressed.	
HYMNS	On feast with proper hymns, when an Office cannot be said in its integrity, e.g, Vespers of a greater feast takes precedence, the hymn is transferred to another greater Hour or joined to its hymn, R. G. XX, 3, e.g. feast of St. Martina 30th January.	Hymns not transferred or joined.	
	Doxology of hymns of iambic metre changed either by occurring season, e.g. Paschaltide *Deo Patri sit gloria* etc., or feast, e.g. of BVM *Jesu, tibi sit gloria* etc.		Doxology of hymns always as printed in the Breviary, not changed at the Hours.

QUI-CUM-QUE	*Quicumque vult*, the "Athanasian Creed" said at Prime on Trinity Sunday and added to the psalms of "green" Sundays when there is no occurring double feast or Octave.	*Quicumque* limited to Prime of Trinity Sunday
NOTES ON MATTINS LESSONS	Sundays (apart from Easter & Pentecost which were treated as feasts): three nocturns of nine lessons. 1st Nocturn: 3 lessons of Scripture (I, II, III) 2nd Nocturn: 3 Patristic lessons (IV, V, VI) 3rd Nocturn: 3 lessons of a homily on the Sunday's Gospel (VII, VIII, IX)	Sundays have a single nocturn of three lessons. 1st lesson: as old lesson I 2nd lesson: old lessons II & III combined. 3rd lesson: old lesson VII.
	D1Cl & D2Cl: three nocturns of nine lessons as Sundays.	Although re-named I Class and II Class, lessons arrangement unaltered.
	Doubles and semi-doubles: three nocturns of nine lessons. 1st Nocturn: 3 lessons of Scripture (I, II, III) 2nd Nocturn: 3 hagiographical (IV, V, VI) 3rd Nocturn: lessons of a homily on the feast's Gospel (VII, VIII, IX)	III Class feasts have a single nocturn of three lessons. 1st lesson: as old lesson I 2nd lesson: old lessons II & III combined. 3rd lesson: "contracted 9th lesson"[19] or lessons IV, V & VI combined.
	Simples: a single nocturn of three lessons. L1: Scripture L2: Scripture L3: Hagiographical for the feast or from the Common.	Commemorations of IV Class days all have lessons from Scripture, no hagiographical material for an occurring commemoration.

NOTES FOR OUTLINE OF CHANGES TO THE ROMAN MISSAL BETWEEN 1955 AND 1962

1 These were the changes to the Calendar, Missal and Breviary resulting from the 1911-13 reform.

2 *Vide: AAS* 52, 1960, pp. 593 seq.

3 Mass *versus populum* was a growing fashion through the 1950s, particularly after it was permitted, in 1957, to add a temporary (freestanding) altar to churches with a single eastward altar already in place.

4 *Vide: Ordo Hebdomadae Sanctae Instauratus, editio typica,* Vatican Polyglot Press, 1956.

5 General decree simplifying the rubrics *Cum nostra hac aetate,* 23 March 1955, *AAS* 47, 1955, pp. 218-224. Tit. II, 1.

6 *Cum nostra* abolished the Vigils of the Epiphany, St. Andrew, the Immaculate Conception, St. Thomas, St. Mathias, St. James, St. Bartholomew, St. Matthew, SS Simon & Jude, and All Saints. Tit. II, 8 & 9.

7 *Cum nostra,* Tit. II, 11.

8 When the Commune Unius aut Plurium Summorum Pontificum was added to the Missal by Pius XII in 1942, it was assigned the Preface of the Apostles. This remained the Preface until '62, when the Common was appointed in its place. Prior to the insertion of the Common of Popes, the Preface of the Apostles was also used "necnon in Missa Creationis et Coronationis Papæ et utriusque Anniversarii" (also changed to the Common Preface in '62). The introduction of the Common of Supreme Pontiff(s) led to the loss of several more or less proper Masses for individual popes as well as a decrease in the frequency of the Common of Martyrs.

9 These feasts were reduced to a commemoration, i.e. just the orations of the feast in the Mass of the feria (weekday), or Christmas Octave, reversing the older arrangement of simple feasts taking precedence over common weekdays.

10 In the old Missal the feast was titled *In Circumcisione DNJC et Octava Nativita.*

11 "Private" Mass had numerous meanings in the older rubrics. In this context it meant a non-conventual Mass.

12 *Vide: Additiones et Variationes, I,* 1 & 2. Prior to 1911-13, outside of collegiate churches only the Mass of the feast would be celebrated with commemoration of the feria or vigil.

13 This limitation has recently been relaxed by a decree of the CDF, *Cum sanctissima,* 25 Mar 2020.

14 E.g. at *Orate fratres, Ritus Servandus* (old) VII, 7; *Sanctus, RS* VII, 8; *Nobis quoque, RS* IX, 3 & *Domine non sum dignus, RS* X, 4.

15 The collects of blessing on February 2 were also changed to short conclusions.

16 E.g, when a saint's feast falls on a "green" Sunday the collect, secret and post-communion of the saint's feast are sung after the respective collect etc. of the Sunday.

17 When a feast is to be commemorated, if it is of double rank, the seasonal prayers are omitted entirely. If the feast is below double rank, the second prayer of the season is omitted; if two saints are commemorated, both seasonal prayers are omitted.

18 *RG* (old) XX, *RS* (old) VIII, 6.

19 *Vide RS* (old) X, 6 and compare with *RS* (new) X, 6.

20 Fortescue, *The Ceremonies of the Roman Rite Described* (Burns & Oates, 1918), 60. Cf. Fortescue-O'Connell, 12th ed. (1962), 73.

21 *RS* (old) X, 6. "Minister autem dextera manu tenens vas cum vino et aqua, sinistra vero mappulum aliquanto post Sacerd. eis porrigit purificationem, et mappulum ad os abstergendum."

NOTES FOR OUTLINE OF CHANGES TO THE ROMAN BREVIARY BETWEEN 1955 AND 1962

1 These were the changes to the Calendar, Missal and Breviary resulting from the 1911-13 reform.

2 In the Office before "1962" the first Sunday of August, September, October and November was the Sunday closest to the 1st of the month e.g. if July 29th were a Sunday that would be the first Sunday of August that year. In the 1962 Breviary the first Sunday of those months was the first Sunday falling within that respective month.

3 General decree simplifying the rubrics *Cum nostra hac aetate*, 23 March 1955, *AAS* 47, 1955, pp. 218-224. Tit. II, 1.

4 *Cum nostra*, Tit. IV, 11.

5 The practice of singing Vespers of the Dead after second Vespers of All Saints (and monthly where it was observed) was abolished and Vespers of the Dead moved to the afternoon of 2nd November.

6 The excising of first Vespers caused some anomalous, and novel, situations: e.g. 9 Aug instead of first Vespers of St. Lawrence the collect of the Vigil is used at ferial Vespers; on Ember Friday in September the Office of the day is used in ferial Vespers. Previously the Office of an Ember Day ended with Mass after None and if ferial Vespers were sung the collect would be of the preceding Sunday.

7 *Cum nostra* abolished the Vigils of the Epiphany, St. Andrew, the Immaculate Conception, St. Thomas, St. Mathias, St. James, St. Bartholomew, St. Matthew, SS Simon & Jude, and All Saints. Tit. II, 8 & 9.

8 *Cum nostra*, Tit. II, 11. (The Sundays within the former Octaves of the Ascension, *Corpus Christi* and the Sacred Heart were celebrated as they had been but without commemoration of the Octave.)

9 Occurrence is when two days, e.g. a feast and a Sunday, fall on the same day. Concurrence is when second Vespers of one liturgical day and first Vespers of the next are reconciled into a single Office. The effect of the 1956 change can be illustrated by example: if the feast of St. Andrew fell on the Monday following Advent 1, before the change Vespers would be first Vespers of the feastday, with commemoration of the Sunday. Post-1956 this is reversed and Vespers are of the Sunday with St. Andrew commemorated. Likewise if the feast of the Annunciation is transferred to the Monday after Low Sunday, before 1956 first Vespers would be of the feast with commemoration of the Sunday, post-1956 *vice versa*.

10 These feasts were reduced to a commemoration, i.e. just the orations of the feast in the Mass of the feria (weekday), or Christmas Octave, reversing the older arrangement of simple feasts taking precedence over common weekdays.

11 In the old Missal the feast was titled *In Circumcisione DNJC et Octava Nativitas*.

12 See table below. In effect most Patristic commentary that had formed second nocturn lessons was abolished.

13 In the Office a commemoration at Lauds and/or Vespers of an occurring lesser Office is formed of the respective antiphon at the *Benedictus/Magnificat*, the ℣ & ℟, and collect.

14 *Cum nostra*, Tit. III, 1 identified "Imperative" commemorations: Sundays, DrCl, days of Advent, Lent, September Ember Days & the Greater Litanies.

15 *Cum nostra*, Tit. IV, 8.

16 *Cum nostra*, Tit. IV, 7.

17 *Cum nostra*, Tit. III, 1 identified 'Imperative' commemorations: Sundays, DrCl, days of Advent, Lent, September Ember Days & the Greater Litanies.

18 With the loss of first Vespers for most feasts in the year, the number of commemorations at Vespers was radically reduced.

19 Following the reform of 1911-13, new editions of the Breviary included a "contracted" lesson consisting of a précis of the IV, V & VI lessons of a feast to be used when the feast was reduced to a commemoration in a higher-ranking Office.

Practical Steps for Transitioning from the 1962 to the Pre-1955 Roman Rite[1]

I. INTRODUCTION

In the summer of 2022, almost as if to mark the first anniversary of the lamentable papal *motu proprio*, Paul Cavendish and Peter Kwasniewski collaborated to produce and publish a much-needed summary[2] of the changes made to the liturgy in three places:

> 1) the simplification of the rubrics outlined in *Cum nostra hac ætate*;
> 2) the introduction of the new rite of Holy Week in *Maxima redemptionis nostræ mysteria*;
> 3) the changes made in the reforms of 1960 and 1962, to the breviary and missal respectively.

This was followed by the publication of Dr. Kwasniewski's *The Once and Future Roman Rite*, where he articulates a fundamental position on the inherently traditional and continuous nature of apostolic liturgy, critiques twentieth-century ruptures, and advocates total restoration of the Roman Rite. Dr. Kwasniewski formally plots the way forward with a final chapter on the pre-1955 liturgy, which deserves our thanks and consideration.

Before proceeding, I should note that this essay takes for granted a reader's knowledge of, or willingness to learn about, the differences in the rubrics.[3]

I have a particular knowledge of the office, above all those hours that would be more routinely prayed in parishes, Vespers and Compline but also Lauds and the minor hours, as I have prayed the 1962 office with some regularity for nine years, and in private, I prayed a combination of *Divino Afflatu*, Tridentine

---

[1] The author of this series wishes to remain anonymous. He is an experienced master of ceremonies and chanter, intimately familiar with both the 1962 rubrics and the pre-1939 rubrics in ordinary parish contexts.
[2] Reproduced as Appendix 2.
[3] A good place to start: www.restorethe54.com/comparisons/.

Compline and festal offices, and a pre-1962 office with the 1962 precedence (Sunday Vespers, with semidoubled antiphons and all but the highest feasts reduced to commemorations); now my circumstances permit me always to use *Divino Afflatu*, so I do.[4]

It is also worth noting in passing that I have only rarely assisted at a Mass with no interpolations whatsoever from a previous edition of the missal; in my experience, a Mass exactly according to 1962 will be celebrated only by American diocesan priests ordained after 2007. I first discovered the traditional Mass via the FSSP, known for preserving the "extra" Confiteor before communion; then in the diocesan parish of my adolescence, the priest bowed to the cross as required. The Institute of Christ the King Sovereign Priest, with which I am most familiar, is famous for "1962 in the hands of Frenchmen" and thus making popular a yet more traditional version of the "rite of Écône," as described by the Rad Trad.[5] In France, even priests who make their bows exclusively to the book are still incensed after the Gospel at sung Mass—J. B. O'Connell could not be clearer in indicating that this is abolished in the 1962 rubrics—and there is virtually always a Confiteor before the distribution of communion.

Also, this essay would not necessarily have been welcomed three or four years ago when it was easier to make changes, yet now many priests will feel pressure to toe the 1962 line lest they lose the right to use even that missal, although, by the same token, now is a favorable time to act. I share their grief and distress, but I hope that they and the members of the flock assisting, such as masters of ceremonies or choirmasters, will read this with ideas for the future, if not for their own strictly private usage away from cameras and the internet, no matter what choice they make in the parishes.

---

[4] By the way, the translated general rubrics of the 1920 missal are also available in a beautifully-prepared PDF (https://sicutincensum.wordpress.com/2020/07/17/pre-62-general-rubrics-of-the-roman-missal/), though the rubrics to the office appear to be lacking; one gets very far, but only so, with a copy of *Learning the Breviary* by Fr. Hausmann, S.J. (not to be confused with *Learning the New Breviary* for the 1960 rubrics—both of which are back in print from Church Latin Publishing Company as of 2025), since the *Additiones et Variationes* to the rubrics of Saint Pius V (under the form known as the Jubilee Rubrics issued in 1900), are what make the *Divino Afflatu* rubrics so complex.

[5] See https://theradtrad.blogspot.com/2015/04/rite-of-gricigliano.html.

It is somewhat trivial to explain why the Roman rite as it existed in 1954 (if not earlier, for reasons to be given below) is the point to which one should return: all of the essential practices are there, albeit with the weekly psalter rearranged by order of Saint Pius X, the antiphons created to accompany this new psalter, and even the new Mass for the feast and octave day of the Assumption instituted by Pope Pius XII. But explaining to someone the extent of the damage even of the 1940s and 1950s is a thirty-minute conversation, without taking into account the flurry of questions from the one listening. A priest of my acquaintance who belongs to a traditional community explained it thusly to a group of young people: "I don't really know the details of the changes." "We pray the 1962 breviary because we're told to do so." These are both reasonable answers given the demands of his apostolic activity and his state in life.

The curious or daring person with some free time could prudently pray according to the 1910 office, then 1911/1954, and finally 1955/1960, in order to see what's up, though looking at a hand missal from the 1940s will be the best most of us can do to see what happened to the Mass in the 1950s and early 1960s.

Precocious laymen might suggest that groups such as the FSSP and especially the Institute of Christ the King Sovereign Priest have erred by sticking to 1962 entirely or by following certain older practices (e.g., the pre-55 Holy Week, the proper doxology of the hymn at Compline, some of the pre-1962 rubrics of the Mass) while following the 1962 calendar and rubrics in everything else.

On the other hand, their priests are subject not only to the bishop but to their superiors, and the parishes they run would attract people who know the difference. On the other hand, a diocesan bishop probably does not know the difference off the top of his head, and while his priests would have more freedom to act, they do not necessarily have the time to do the research and to transition the TLM community towards a more traditional observance.

Or do they? Can this be done? I believe it is possible, with careful planning and consideration both of the higher-level stakes (Rome, the bishop...) and of lower-level ones (the needs of the faithful).

In a parish well-known to this author, the pastor arrived and continued to follow the 1962 calendar (especially the precedence of Sundays over virtually all feasts), although the prayers at the foot of the altar and Last Gospel were always recited, even on days when the '62 missal had removed them. Vespers strictly followed the 1962 rubrics, with the commemorations made according to the same.

Slowly but surely, suppressed feasts, like those of the first week in May (suppressed in 1960 as duplicates), came back along with vigils, like that of All Saints said the day before the feast. The Credo was restored to the feasts which previously required it before 1955 and 1960. Holy Week and the Pentecost vigil came back immediately; there is simply no reason to stick with the reformed versions (especially that of Pius XII, but also that of Paul VI) if you really believe it is worth reviving the traditional form of the Roman Rite. The priest introduced proper Last Gospels said on Sundays where the feast impedes a Sunday Mass or on certain other occasions required by the rubrics, then seasonal commemorations at Mass (that is, the prayers said after the main oration), and those of feasts; one of the genius aspects of the reforms of Pius X is this legal fiction elevating Sundays over most, but not all, feasts. Finally, the suffrages (the antiphon, versicle, and collect said per the rubrics: one is of "All Saints" sung most of the year; the other said in Paschal Time is "of the cross"), then sanctoral commemorations (most all of the saints on Saturday evening and on Sunday are just dropped under 1962), and now semidoubled antiphons (intoned to the asterisk, followed by the psalm, then sung in full after the psalm) along with the precedence of the *Divino Afflatu* rubrics have been restored at Vespers.

So that's what happened in this parish: a pretty full restoration of the Roman Rite. How, then, does one get there?

In the next three parts, we will look at the Mass, the Office, and the question of Posture. I shall refrain from a detailed treatment of the pontifical ceremonies, since that depends on acquiring a suitable pontifical and a willing bishop (already difficult enough), and the scope is simply too grand for the task at hand.

Such a transition can sometimes be confusing, as much as for the priest as for the faithful, and one would do well to briefly instruct from the pulpit and in the bulletin or at other appropriate times, such as on Saturday mornings, where there is more time to consider the finer details. Priests should remember that, while one must be "all things to all men," one should never act as if the audience is unintelligent and cannot, through some work, come to learn and appreciate these details according to their capacities.

2. THE MASS

Before any kind of work can begin in earnest, one must use an ordo alongside the old books of liturgy and try to learn the rubrics. The well-established Saint Lawrence Press Ordo[6] is slightly different from the web-based Ordo of *Restore the '54*,[7] which has the new Assumption and Immaculate Heart offices, the Common of Holy Popes, and some changes to the calendar, like the feast of the Queenship of Mary on May 31, which bumps Saint Angela Merici to the next day. This is not a terribly important feast, but the problem is now that a new double of the II class interrupts a week routinely filled with some feasts: the Ascension, Pentecost, Trinity, etc. routinely fall on or around this day, and as a double of the II class, it eventually is transferred to a free day.

One could also simply ignore all but the changes to the Assumption and its octave and call it a day, as the Immaculate Heart Mass has become beloved among Catholics attached to not just the liturgy but to the devotional culture of the immediate pre-conciliar era. While keeping Our Lady's request to honor her Immaculate Heart on five first Saturdays is not something which I treat frivolously, nevertheless, she did not say that it must be with the votive Mass of the Immaculate Heart.

Attention must also be called to the rubrics of votive Masses, somewhat different than the 1962 rubrics, though not challenging as the SLP Ordo has a handy chart. The trouble is that a Requiem Mass or a votive Mass said on more solemn occasions (so, something more complex than the replacement of the ferial Mass per annum when votive Masses are permitted) have special rubrics for the orations, the Gloria, the Credo, and the precedence, all of which are vastly different from the 1962 rubrics, which are not necessarily straightforward or simple as it is.

If one has a sufficient command of French, then referencing the *Manuel de liturgie et cérémonial selon le rit romain* of Stercky[8] (taking over for Le Vavasseur) is indispensable in addition to the original Fortescue.[9] These volumes are far more comprehensive

---

[6] See http://ordorecitandi.blogspot.com.

[7] See http://restorethe54.com.

[8] See https://archive.org/details/ManuelDeLiturgieSterckyTomeI/. Volume 2 of Stercky may be found at https://archive.org/details/ManuelDeLiturgie SterckyTomeII/ (note the subtle difference in link: only the final letter).

[9] See https://archive.org/details/ceremoniesofromaoofort/mode/2up.

than Fortescue(-O'Connell) and O'Connell combined, and the work should have been entirely translated a long time ago; they merit republication in French as well. Note that an excerpt in translation entitled *Sacrificare: Ceremonies of Low Mass* was published in 1946 and is currently available in a print-on-demand edition,[10] though it deserves a proper reprint from a reputable publishing house.

In all cases, it is perfectly wise to begin with the little details: the name of Saint Joseph is not in the canon. One can immediately begin bowing to the cross as required at the epistle corner; using the three tones of voice and two kinds of head bows and bows of the body; always reciting the prayers at the foot of the altar and the Last Gospel — mostly the ordinary one from Saint John; praying the Confiteor before communion; finally, incensing the celebrant of a sung Mass after the Gospel.[11]

Additionally, the priest should simply not sit down, and should rise a little earlier, in order to read the epistle and gospel at solemn Mass, which essentially no one will mind; the faithful are listening to the chants. Finally, the priest should follow the traditional rubrics as to which tones of the Preface and the Pater Noster should be used, which happen to neatly correspond to the new categories of the 1962 office (in particular, simples are commemorations, simple votive Masses are IV class, and nothing else changes).

The pastor should also strive to say Mass *pro populo* on the required days, a table of which would be found in the various books covering the subject. Treating holy days, even suppressed ones, as something special is almost entirely lost, and this will have to be recovered as well. "Why can't I have Mass said for Grandma Anne and Grandpa Lawrence on their name days?" Well, because the church considers saying Mass for the people under the pastor's care one of his most important duties.

---

[10] See www.lulu.com/shop/louis-stercky/sacrificare/paperback/product-q8eew4.html.

[11] This one is more controversial, as not every place received an indult for incense at sung Mass before the 1962 rubrics made it universal. But it is the expectation the world over, and even if a sung Mass is closer in many ways to a low Mass than to a solemn Mass, it seems that any step today that would result in detaching sung Mass from solemn Mass is a step in the wrong direction.

One can add the Credo for Apostles, Doctors, Saint Mary Magdalene, and the Holy Angels without touching the calendar or precedence and without making any other commemorations. Since there is already a preface of the Blessed Sacrament, the preface of the Nativity on Corpus Christi celebrated on Thursday or as an external solemnity can be used without difficulty, as there is already the possibility of avoiding the common preface or, on Sunday, that of the Trinity, and virtually no one would blink if the same preface was used on the Transfiguration.

As far as more significant changes go, I would of course start with Holy Week and the vigil of Pentecost. A wealth of material exists such that the rite can be celebrated correctly and with dignity; I am no fan of broadcasting all liturgies, but 2020 provided proof that you can celebrate the traditional rite in a parish church with a skeleton crew. It is also true that the most numerous and momentous reformatory changes occurred with these days of the liturgical year, meaning it's impossible to mix-and-match old and new (i.e., pre-55 and 1955-1969) in a satisfactory way.

Nevertheless, if one must be incrementalist, then the easiest place to begin is on Holy Thursday, where the rubrics of Mass would deviate only for the ministers, not for the schola (aside from the Agnus Dei, where the *change* from the ordinary way is in the Pian rite, not that which came before or after) or for the faithful, and at Tenebræ, usually anticipated as it is. Psalm 50 is still right there in the books, and the *strepitus* (the fun part, the noise at the end) is essentially never omitted. Good Friday is perhaps the next change, given that the day is unique no matter what, followed by the two more complex and very notably different days, Palm Sunday and Holy Saturday.

Further, if you obtain folded chasubles for Holy Week, then you can use them the rest of the year, starting with Candlemas, to which minimal changes were made and which only apply after Septuagesima, which means that only the vestments change (except once every few years).

Replacing "Ite, missa est" with "Benedicamus Domino" in Advent and Lent or on the Ember Days of September, then adding proper Last Gospels on penitential weekdays where the festal Mass is said instead (even without touching the 1962 rubrics of the Lenten calendar precedence! — one thinks of Saint Joseph, the Annunciation, the privileged votive Masses, proper first-class feasts, and the Masses now permitted by the decree *Cum Sanctissima*), would be easy steps to take next, followed by the reintroduction of proper Last Gospels whenever they occur, including when a feast falls on an ordinary Sunday. One might wish to begin earlier with Christmas day, given that its Gospel is already Saint John's prologue and would otherwise have no Last Gospel. Can anyone protest too much? In fact, the Ordinariate has this privilege!

By the way, there is virtually no reason to ever justify the short form of Ember Saturday's liturgy, no matter what rubrics one uses otherwise.

The commemorations of the Mass should be added progressively according to the difficulty for the celebrant and the people. These are straightforward on double feasts or when a double feast is simplified due to the Sunday: pray the collects of the (other) saints, then move to the epistle, unless there is an *oratio imperata* to be prayed by the order of the bishop or other authority (rare if not nonexistent outside of certain traditional communities).

It can become much more complicated at a votive Mass, including the "daily" Requiem Mass which has three orations; when a semidouble or simplex feast is commemorated; or during octaves or other occasions which have different prayers than those of the season (e.g., a day within the octave of All Saints has different prayers than the ones assigned for the time after Pentecost).

More will be said about these with respect to the office, but suffice it to say that one could start on the rare occasions when one makes only the commemorations of the season, gradually moving to commemorate feasts, both of which can already be done, at least in a limited way, at a 1962-compliant low Mass. It is probably unwise to start with Sundays or feasts with four collects, e.g., on June 26, 2022, the Sunday within the octave of the Sacred Heart, when, in pre-55 land, collects would be sung of the Third Sunday after Pentecost, of several martyrs, of the Octave of the Lord, and of the Octave of Saint John the Baptist.

That leaves the calendar itself and the other rubrics. Start with the "votive" Mass of the suppressed feasts, all found in the 1962 missal's Masses for Various Places; the feast of Saint Joseph in Paschaltide is the votive Mass of Saint Joseph, so one could usually say this Mass on the third Wednesday of Eastertide without fuss.

If the feast of an Apostle or another II class feast falls on a Sunday and would have taken its place before 1962, one should follow that precedence, commemorating Sunday appropriately. Also, move the Apostles to Monday if there is a conflict, as is the case when October 28 falls on the Sunday which is the feast of Christ the King or when Saint Matthias falls on a Sunday of Lent.

The full vigils, including that of the Epiphany, will have to be restored last, if one does not already possess a pre-1955 missal. The same holds for the octaves which have proper texts for all or some of the days (in particular, the days within the octave of Saints Peter and Paul), but the Second and Third Sundays after Pentecost have no textual changes not found in a 1962 missal and can be restored quickly as the Sundays within the respective octaves of the Lord.

The pre-1939 recension is imperfect. It would perhaps be better, at conventual Mass, to celebrate ancient vigils instead of later feasts (on June 28, the vigil of Saints Peter and Paul and variously the feast of Saint Irenaeus or of Pope Saint Leo II) and on August 9 (the vigil of Saint Lawrence and the feast of the Curé d'Ars). Instituting the vigil and suppressing or moving around feasts (again), or removing the vigil in the 1960 liturgy, came at the cost of everything else, and a change to permit the vigil at conventual Mass (without having to duplicate the festal Mass) would have mirrored the rubrics for private Masses (I take the meaning of "private" to be the Mass said outside of the parish schedule, not as the "parochial Mass" in lieu of a conventual Mass where there is no community — the sort of Mass, in other words, that priests say right after Lauds in the monastery). Those allowed priests to choose the Mass ad libitum when a vigil or ferial day of Lent, or the Ember Days, was to be said, although public Masses, including the main Mass, really ought to be of the feast.[12]

One final change: the Mass of the Rogation days has a unique Alleluia in the pre-1962 missal; the Alleluia with the verse *Laudate Dominum* is sung, but the form is not responsorial. Two Alleluias are sung as on other days of Paschal Time in the 1962 missal, for consistency.

Surveying the many differences listed above, we should bear in mind that there is no one order that must be followed in

---

[12] As an aside, the term "private Mass" is nebulous, having at least eight definitions and has consequences if the priest is saying a community Mass for his community, conventual or otherwise, or as the main parochial Mass. As noted earlier, a pastor would have had to say Mass *pro populo* on many feast days according to the former law.

implementing them, nor a prescribed pace at which to move. The changes to be implemented in parallel with one's breviary (to be described in the next section) can be mixed and matched. The order I have suggested, however, seems to be a good general order that makes logical sense. At a minimum, I have tried to lay out each element that will need to be restored to the traditional Roman Mass.

3. THE DIVINE OFFICE

Before now, I have hinted at reasons for returning to the 1939 office rather than the 1954 form (which happens to have a memorable rhyming slogan in English: "restore the '54"). For Holy Week, there were no significant changes prior to 1955, so any edition will do; but as for the calendar, the pontifical (not treated here), and the office, the 1939 status has much to commend it. Let me offer one concrete example of a treasure found in older editions that is harmed as time goes on.

The Canticle of Canticles is primarily read at Matins of the Assumption octave, in an orderly manner over the eight days. (Some chapters are omitted due to the introduction of double feasts, but those could be omitted or the rubrics amended to require the readings of the octave, instead of the occurring Scripture.) In any case, under the 1950 office, chapter 1 of Canticles is no longer read; chapter 2 is still read, but on the Visitation, a less important feast added much later (although it is a feast commemorating a Scriptural event); chapter 3 is omitted if Saint Mary Magdalene is impeded (and 1960 omits even that), and chapter 8 is now omitted in the office of the Immaculate Heart of Mary. Chapter 4 is read as the day is unimpeded on the general calendar, and the rest are omitted due to feasts as mentioned above. There is also no reason to read something written by the reigning pope in the office of one of the greatest Marian feasts. But let us move on to the transition, of which this series is supposed to be a guide.

The challenge of making changes in an entire community remains, and these are felt most acutely with the choir office, particularly if some of the office is sung in choir and the rest said privately. Thankfully, that is above my pay grade. Some suggestions for the reform of the office, and to an extent the Mass, are also applicable to priests belonging to a diocese and should be noted; in his own breviary, the diocesan priest might simply take up the whole old office, at least for the minor hours, working up to the full Lauds and Vespers, then Matins.

The simplest place to begin would be by praying the suppressed silent prayers before and after the Hours, which are in the 1962 breviary as it is, can be put on a card, or are easily memorized; the Marian antiphon could then be added to the end of Lauds or the final day hour when said in a bunch following Lauds, or when Vespers is separated from Compline (and when no other pious exercise, sermon, or Benediction follows). Surely no cleric would decline the opportunity to invoke his Mother's protection more often?

Clerics in major orders (from the diaconate, if transitional, or according to the community's constitutions, from the subdiaconate) who are obliged to pray the entire office could add the first psalm omitted at Lauds of penitential days to Prime, at least in private, though this may pose some difficulties for clerics who pray Prime with community members who are not so bound. That psalm is still in the breviary, and so are the suppressed verses of psalm 88 cut from Christmas, the Transfiguration, or Christ the King, whereas the canticle of Deuteronomy at Saturday Lauds is mutilated such that one could not pray the full text from a 1962 breviary.

From there, the clergy praying the full office could semidouble the antiphons of the minor hours and of Compline, including those sung with members who are not yet subdeacons (typically Prime, Terce, or Sext and Compline); the ferial preces could be prayed anytime the penitential Lauds are said or Vespers are of the feria of Advent or Lent. This change does not even affect the entire year, nor even every day within the seasons.

For those lucky enough to use older, original versions of the *Liber Usualis* in choir, praying the doxologies as printed for Compline is easy to implement without much thought, as the book is written that way! This would also apply to the other minor hours, of course, although the doxologies are rarely printed for offices other than festal Compline; for example, one has to learn that it changes during the season of Easter or on feasts (an asterisk printed in the breviary reminds the cleric of this).

Semidoubling the hours on Sundays (perhaps surprisingly, all Sundays are privileged but of semidouble rite, except for Low Sunday, which is double major, and the Sundays that are feasts, i.e., Easter and Pentecost, as well as Trinity, Christ the King, etc., fixed on Sunday) and at daily Compline (sometimes prayed with the faithful) is another easy step to take at public offices. Saint-Eugène-Sainte-Cécile in Paris already does this for most Sundays, and frankly it is easier anyway if you are introducing Vespers, since the psalm matches what is printed for the antiphon, particularly with Psalm 109; the priest intones the antiphon, which is the first words of the psalm, so the cantors continue with the psalm. At first, you could still follow the 1962 observance in omitting the commemorations and suffrages. Adding commemorations and suffrages according to the rubrics and the occurrences or concurrences of the calendar (including the Incarnation doxology for the commemoration of a lesser Marian feast) would be the last step.

That said, the commemorations can be somewhat complicated, particularly when octaves get involved, and figuring out the order is not always intuitive; one simply has to trust the Ordo while trying to learn the rubrics on the fly. For example, the order of commemorations for June 19, 2022 (Sunday within the octave of Corpus Christi) was complicated by the commemoration of the octave, and this is a point of the rubrics that was changed in 1911 to be more complicated than before, leaving it to be blown up in 1955 and in 1960.

For priests belonging to a traditional community, it would be better to work commemorations out privately and to mutually agree on them—say, starting at the community's seminary—than to introduce them independently, with disagreements arising in different churches; the commemorations in the office can be easy to forget or to execute incorrectly as well, as the rubrics for "Oremus" and the conclusions are not the same as at Mass. At the office, the celebrant sings "Oremus" before each collect, but this is not the case at Mass: it is sung before the first collect and then before the second, but not before subsequent collects. (I recommend a sticky note or an index card.)

In lieu of worrying about that first, restoring I Vespers where there is no conflict seems to be a more prudent choice; to pick at low-hanging fruit, Vespers of the Vigil of Saint Lawrence is an anomaly easily fixed by saying I Vespers of the feast provided in the 1960 breviary. I would also suggest singing the traditional hymns of Vespers and Lauds of the Assumption, even with the 1950 collect and chapter for expediency, before moving on to the traditional prayers down the road.

Next, psalms for the feast should replace the ferial psalms of the minor hours on II class feasts. One would already have the necessary texts since the antiphons are from the Lauds already prayed, from the common or proper. Then one can celebrate I Vespers of all II class feasts, especially the feasts of Apostles, and add the commemorations of lower feasts (in occurrence at Lauds and, at first, in concurrence at Vespers, and going from there).

After this begins a different kind of challenge: restoring texts that simply do not exist in a 1962 breviary or which would constitute a greater burden. The *preces* at the minor hours and the dominical *preces* of Prime and Compline are very short, but they were either removed or would require substantial pencil markings in a 1962 breviary if you wish to say them. The same is true for the suffrages. Praying Vespers of the Dead after canonical Vespers of All Saints on November 1 is trivial in the sense that the text is in the breviary, but praying two Vespers is an utterly foreign concept, and when Vespers of the dead is prayed on certain occasions, psalms are added towards the end which are found in the breviary, just not in the 1960 office of the dead. In other words, get a pencil.

Changing the chapter and the verse at Prime when called for by the older rubrics is simple enough and adds virtually no time to the office, but the texts would not necessarily be in a 1962 breviary (in fact, they mostly are not). Also, commemorating a lesser Marian feast at Saturday or Sunday Vespers requires memorizing the doxology if using a breviary (easy enough, admittedly); at least in all cases, one needs to create the chant score if using a *Liber Usualis.* (The omission of the doxology for all tones of the hymns where this happens on green Sundays, from Saturday evening to that of Sunday, is a strange lacuna.)

Unfortunately, restoring Matins is probably the last significant step to take, because the readings, especially on Sundays, cannot be reconstituted from a 1962 breviary; you have to have an earlier edition, or, less ideally, your phone or a document created with the missing portions, but the thing is that the readings are not that long. Efficiently praying Matins with Lauds on a feast of nine lessons takes less than an hour; even taking into consideration apostolic demands, does one not have an hour to watch and pray? If not, we should fix this, and the faithful should support priests doing this according to their own abilities. (Both are easier said than done.)

Praying Matins is all the more easy considering the compromise psalter, of which the flaws are evident after only a few days of praying the Roman office of 1911/1954 (such as on July 9 and 10, 2022, with Our Lady on Saturday followed by a green Sunday with no doubles commemorated on either day). Nevertheless, the secular clergy would consider this office the most burdensome, not entirely without reason.

In contrast, praying the Athanasian Creed is, in theory, not especially burdensome for those who must pray Prime, but it does require paying attention to the commemorations of octaves and double feasts (these suppress the recitation of this creed) such that its reintroduction could come before adding commemorations at Mass or at the same time, depending on whether one is in a community that should try to pray in the same way or if one is alone (or with other diocesan priests) in a parish. In other words, one could accelerate the restoration of one's office at the same pace as, or a faster pace than, that of the public Mass. *Mutatis mutandis* for the suffrages already mentioned in the context of Vespers, which also occur, even more often, at Lauds.

4. POSTURES AND THE GUISE OF A CONCLUSION

While there are no strict rubrics for the lay faithful, virtually all authorities (such as editors of hand missals and of ceremonials) agreed that if the people are to do anything, they should follow the rubrics for the clerics. In other words, rubrics are normative, if not strictly binding. It would be especially good to work on the posture of the acolytes which goes hand-in-hand with that of the choir at key moments like the Canon or the orations on certain days of the year, most often at the Requiem Mass, since this is sung more often in parishes than the ferial Masses. This in turn will influence the people's gestures such that they correspond better to the liturgical action, better drawing the distinction between festal or dominical and penitential.

But there is one rubric that does demand attention. The liturgical books could not be clearer that, on Good Friday, the priest, the ministers, and servers take off their shoes and proceed to the back. They genuflect on both knees and bow three times before kissing the cross. The faithful do exactly the same. This is something that was detested by Thomas Cranmer at the English Reformation; we would do well to carry out perhaps the most elaborate form of adoration in the Roman rite, which is not known (unlike the Byzantine liturgy) for its full-body prostrations.

As to the last elements to be restored, the pontifical ceremonies and the *Ritual*, the former is out of pastors' hands unless they find a willing bishop, although the pontifical Mass itself has very few changes except for those made in the entire 1962 liturgy, e.g. the deletion of the Judica me, etc. on certain days. The *Pontificale Romanum* and the *Cæremoniale Episcoporum* govern that form of the Mass to which no changes were made, apparently due to error or negligence on the part of Rome. Thus, one is unquestionably free to celebrate using these older books. Plus, you either do a pontifical ceremony, or you do nothing. There is no middle ground of transition.

The *Ritual* presents particular challenges, since the vernacular editions were sometimes substantially different in the 1950s and in 1962, and the permissions granted to all priests (versus bishops or religious of an order or congregation) did not exist before; however, if one acquiesces to using the Latin alone, then one can use virtually any edition for the ordinary prayers and blessings; those seriously interested should follow the Hand Missal History project,[13] which promises to detail the history of the vernacular in the rituals over the last several centuries.

It bears repeating that there is no one pace to match, no schedule to follow, although I personally think that the order outlined here is sound and can be adapted most easily to the needs of parishes, religious communities, and seminaries of societies of apostolic life, for private usage if not public usage in these difficult times. It's not my neck on the block, so moving glacially would not especially disturb me, although I hope that the actual experience of celebrating the traditional Holy Week, or even watching it online, and reading articles and books on the pre-55 Roman Rite, has by now convinced even the most reluctant traditional or trad-adjacent priest of the supremacy of the majestic traditional Roman Rite celebrated without the ever-accelerating and ever-burgeoning changes of the twentieth century.

I should address some final concerns. I advocate for celebrating the pre-Pius XII liturgy because it is the fullest approved expression of the Roman rite following the reforms of Saint Pius X; this

---

[13] See https://handmissalhistory.com/.

is important, because the John XXIII breviary has at its heart the Pius X psalter. This is the familiar office for traditionally-minded clergy, and there are many beloved things in these liturgical books, particularly the 1927 Mass and office of the Sacred Heart.

In addressing arguments from both progressives and conservatives, we acknowledge that the 1960 rubrics have the flaws which we already criticize in the *Novus Ordo*. These flaws prompt us to take up the non-deformed books, yet without being in a situation where we are, as it were, making things up on the fly, as we go along; for that would be just a different version of tinkeritis or optionitis.

Integrity is important; we should not try to make up a new calendar, a new system of precedence, or a new breviary with the Jubilee rubrics of 1900 (and so, with the historical *cursus psalmorum*) — on our own authority. We should not follow some hybrid forever out of mere convenience, or flip-flop between rubrics. Those who are serious should restore the ceremonies and follow the rubrics of a definite edition such as the 1939 missal, and then stick to it.

In case this was not clear, I reiterate that the times are strange, if not dangerous. Who knows what will happen tomorrow; this is an evergreen question, but with certain technological developments, both bishops and Roman curial officials can, and do, micromanage, with ease. Nor should people do things which will gravely offend the authorities in question or which require disobedience in a sort of slimy way. I encourage people — the clergy above all — to do these things *quietly* and with great love for the Lord and for their people, but without dissimulation or other troublesome behaviors that cannot bring victory.

I pray that one day, every community that currently uses or has previously used the *usus antiquior* will one day be able to do so according to the integral editions, when the right moment comes. Until then, we take it step by step, brick by brick.

APPENDIX 4

Translations of Key
Liturgical Documents

PIUS V, *QUO PRIMUM* (1570)[1]

Pius, Bishop, Servant of the Servants of God, for a Perpetual Memorial of the Matter.

Upon Our elevation to the Apostolic throne, We gladly turned Our mind and energies, and directed all Our thoughts, to the matter of preserving incorrupt the public worship of the Church; and We have striven, with God's help, by every means in Our power to achieve that purpose.

Whereas amongst other decrees of the holy Council of Trent, We were charged with revision and re-issue of the sacred books, to wit, the Catechism, the Missal and the Breviary; and whereas We have with God's consent published a Catechism for the instruction of the faithful and thoroughly revised the Breviary for the due performance of the Divine Office, We next, in order that the Missal and Breviary might be in perfect harmony, as is right and proper (considering that it is altogether fitting that there should be in the Church only one appropriate manner of Psalmody and one sole rite of celebrating Mass), deemed it necessary to give Our immediate attention to what still remained to be done, namely the re-editing of the Missal with the least possible delay.

We resolved accordingly to delegate this task to select erudite men; and they, having at every stage of their work and with the utmost care collated the ancient codices in Our Vatican Library and reliable (original or amended) codices from elsewhere, and having also consulted the writing of ancient and approved authors who have bequeathed to us records relating to the said sacred rites, thus restored the Missal itself to the pristine norm and rite of the holy Fathers. When this production had been subjected to close scrutiny and further amended, We, after mature consideration, ordered that the final result be forthwith printed and published in Rome, so that all may enjoy the fruit of this labor; that priests

---

[1] Translation by John Warrington, www.newadvent.org/library/docs_pio5qp.htm.

may know what prayers to use, and what rites and ceremonies they are to observe henceforward in the celebration of Masses.

Now therefore, in order that all everywhere may adopt and observe what has been delivered to them by the Holy Roman Church, Mother and Mistress of the other churches, it shall be unlawful henceforth and forever throughout the Christian world to sing or to read Masses according to any formula other than that of this Missal published by Us; this ordinance is to apply to all churches and chapels, with or without care of souls, patriarchal, collegiate, and parochial, be they secular or belonging to any religious Order, whether of men (including the military Orders) or of women, in which conventual Masses are or ought to be sung aloud in choir or read privately according to the rites and customs of the Roman Church; to apply, moreover, even if the said churches have been in any way exempted, whether by indult of the Apostolic See, by custom, by privilege, or even by oath or Apostolic confirmation, or have their rights and faculties guaranteed to them in any other way whatsoever, saving only those in which the practice of saying Mass differently was granted over 200 years ago simultaneously with the Apostolic See's institution and confirmation of the church, and those in which there has prevailed a similar custom followed continuously for a period of not less than 200 years; in which cases We in no wise rescind their prerogatives or customs aforesaid. Nevertheless, if this Missal which We have seen fit to publish be more agreeable to these last, We hereby permit them to celebrate Mass according to its rite, subject to the consent of their bishop or prelate and of their whole Chapter, all else to the contrary notwithstanding. All other churches aforesaid are hereby denied the use of other missals, which are to be wholly and entirely rejected; and by this present Constitution, which shall have the force of law in perpetuity, We order and enjoin under pain of Our displeasure that nothing be added to Our newly published Missal, nothing omitted therefrom, and nothing whatsoever altered therein.

We specifically command each and every patriarch, administrator and all other persons of whatsoever ecclesiastical dignity, be they even Cardinals of the Holy Roman Church or possessed of any other rank or pre-eminence, and We order them, by virtue of holy obedience, to sing or to read the Mass according to the rite and manner and norm herein laid down by Us, and henceforward to discontinue and utterly discard all other rubrics and rites of other missals, howsoever ancient, which they have been accustomed to follow, and not to presume in celebrating Mass to introduce any ceremonies or recite any prayers other than those contained in this Missal.

Furthermore, by these presents and by virtue of Our Apostolic authority We give and grant in perpetuity that for the singing or reading of Mass in any church whatsoever, this Missal may be followed absolutely, without any scruple of conscience or fear of incurring any penalty, judgment, or censure, and may be freely and lawfully used. Nor shall bishops, administrators, canons, chaplains, and other secular priests, or religious of whatsoever Order or by whatsoever title designated, be obliged to celebrate Mass otherwise than enjoined by Us. We likewise order and declare that no one whosoever shall be forced or coerced into altering this Missal and that this present Constitution can never be revoked or modified, but shall forever remain valid and have the force of law, notwithstanding previous constitutions or edicts of provincial or synodal councils, and notwithstanding the usage of the churches aforesaid, established by very long and even immemorial prescription, saving only usage of more than 200 years.

Consequently it is Our will, and by the same authority We decree, that one month after publication of this Our constitution and Missal, priests of the Roman Curia shall be obliged to sing or to read the Mass in accordance therewith; others south of the Alps, after three months; those who live beyond the Alps, after six months or as soon as the Missal becomes available for purchase.

Furthermore, in order that the said Missal may be preserved incorrupt and kept free from defects and errors, the penalty for non-observance in the case of all printers resident in territory directly or indirectly subject to Ourselves and the Holy Roman Church shall be forfeiture of their books and a fine of one hundred gold ducats payable by that very fact to the Apostolic Treasury. In the case of those resident in other parts of the world, it shall be automatically excommunication and other penalties at Our discretion; and by Our Apostolic authority and the tenor of these presents, We also decree that they must not dare or presume either to print or to publish or to sell, or in any way to take delivery of such books without Our approval and consent, or without express permission of the Apostolic Commissary in the said parts appointed by Us for that purpose. Each of the said printers must receive from the aforementioned Commissary a standard Missal to serve as an exemplar and agree faithfully therewith, varying in no wise from the first impression printed in Rome.

But, since it would be difficult for this present Constitution to be transmitted to all parts of the world and to come to the notice of all concerned simultaneously, We direct that it be, as usual, posted and published at the doors of the Basilica of the Prince of Apostles, at those of the Apostolic Chancery, and at the end of the Campo dei Fiori; moreover, We direct that printed copies of the same, signed by a notary public and authenticated with the seal of an ecclesiastical dignitary, shall possess the same unqualified and indubitable validity everywhere and in every country that would attend the display there of Our present text. Accordingly, no one whosoever is permitted to infringe or rashly contravene this notice of Our permission, statute, ordinance, command, direction, grant, indult, declaration, will, decree, and prohibition. Should any person venture to do so, let him understand that he will incur the wrath of Almighty God and of the blessed Apostles Peter and Paul.

Given at St. Peter's, Rome, in the year of Our Lord's Incarnation one thousand five hundred and seventy, on the fourteenth day of July in the fifth year of Our Pontificate.

PIUS V, *QUOD A NOBIS* (1568)[2]

Pius, Bishop, Servant of the Servants of God.

Obliged by the duty of Our pastoral office to devote all Our care to ensuring, as far as We are able with the help of God, the implementation of the decrees of the Council of Trent, We feel all the more bound to this in matters that directly concern the glory of God and the special obligations of ecclesiastical persons. Among these matters, We place at the forefront the sacred prayers, praises, and acts of thanksgiving contained in the Roman Breviary. This form of the Divine Office, once piously and wisely established by the Sovereign Pontiffs Gelasius I and Gregory I, and later reformed by Gregory VII, having over time deviated from its ancient institution, it has become necessary to restore it once more to the ancient rule of prayer. Indeed, some have disfigured

---

[2] Vincent Petit, *Église et Nation: La Question Liturgique en France au XIXe Siècle* (Presses Universitaires de Rennes, 2010), 125.

the harmonious structure of the ancient Breviary, mutilating it in many places and altering it by the addition of many uncertain and novel elements. Others, in great numbers, drawn by greater convenience, eagerly adopted the new and abbreviated Breviary composed by Francisco de Quiñones, Cardinal-Priest of the Title of Santa Croce in Gerusalemme. Moreover, a detestable custom had crept into the provinces, namely, that in churches which from their foundation had the practice of reciting and chanting the Canonical Hours according to the ancient Roman custom, as well as others, each bishop created his own particular Breviary, thereby tearing apart, through these new and dissimilar offices — specific, as it were, to each diocese — that communion which consists in offering prayers and praises to the same God in one and the same form. Hence, in so many places, the disruption of divine worship; hence, among the clergy, ignorance of ecclesiastical ceremonies and rites, so that countless ministers of the Church performed their duties indecently, to the great scandal of the devout.

Paul IV, of happy memory, deeply grieved by this diversity in the Divine Office, resolved to remedy it. To this end, after taking measures to prohibit the future use of the new Breviary, he undertook to restore the form of the Canonical Hours to its ancient form and institution. But having departed this life before completing what he had so excellently begun, and the Council of Trent, after several interruptions, having been resumed by Pius IV, of pious memory, the Fathers, assembled for a salutary reform, judged that the Breviary should be restored according to the plan of the same Paul IV. Therefore, all that had been collected and prepared by this Pontiff for this purpose was sent by the aforementioned Pope Pius to the Fathers of the Council assembled at Trent. The Council, having entrusted the revision of the Breviary to several learned and pious men in addition to their other duties, and the conclusion of the said Council being near, the assembly, by decree, referred the matter to the authority and judgment of the Roman Pontiff. He, having summoned to Rome those Fathers designated for this task and having joined to them several suitable persons from the same city, undertook to bring this work to completion.

But this Pope himself having entered the way of all flesh, and We, by the disposition of divine mercy, having been raised, though unworthy, to the summit of the Apostolate, We have pursued with the greatest zeal the completion of this sacred work, even calling upon the assistance of other skilled persons. And today, by the great mercy of God (for so We understand it), We have the happiness of seeing this Roman Breviary finally completed. Having repeatedly examined the method followed by those We appointed to this task; having seen that, in carrying out their work, they did not deviate from the ancient Breviaries of the most illustrious churches of Rome and of Our Vatican Library; that they followed the most authoritative authors on this subject; and that, while removing foreign and uncertain elements, they omitted nothing essential to the proper structure of the ancient Divine Office; We have approved their work and ordered it to be printed in Rome and disseminated everywhere. Therefore, that this measure may take effect, by the authority of these presents, We first revoke and abolish the new Breviary composed by the said Cardinal Francisco, in whatever church, monastery, convent, order, military order, or place, whether of men or women, even exempt, it may have been permitted by the Apostolic See, whether from its first institution or otherwise.

Moreover, We abolish all other Breviaries, whether older than the aforementioned or granted any privilege whatsoever, or promulgated by bishops in their dioceses, and We forbid their use in all churches of the world, monasteries, convents, military orders, orders, and places, whether of men or women, even exempt, in which the Divine Office is customarily or obligatorily celebrated according to the rite of the Roman Church; excepting, however, those churches which, by virtue of an original institution approved by the Apostolic See, or by custom, both dating back more than two hundred years, have a clear practice of using a certain Breviary. To these, We do not intend to remove the ancient right to recite and chant their Office, but We permit them, if they so prefer, to recite and chant in choir the Breviary We now promulgate, provided that the bishop and the entire chapter consent.

We entirely revoke each and every apostolic and other permission, custom, statute, even if confirmed by oath, apostolic confirmation, or any other means; privileges, licenses, and indults to pray and chant, both in choir and outside, according to the usage and rites of the thus-suppressed Breviaries, granted to the aforementioned churches, monasteries, convents, military orders, orders, and places, or to the cardinals of the Holy Roman Church, patriarchs, archbishops, bishops, abbots, and other prelates of the Churches;

and finally, to all other ecclesiastical persons, secular and regular, of either sex, for whatever reason; even if approved and renewed, in whatever form they may be conceived and by whatever decrees and clauses they may be corroborated; and We decree that henceforth all these things shall lose their force and effect.

Having thus forbidden the use of any other Breviary, We order that Our Breviary and form of prayer and chanting be observed in all churches throughout the world, monasteries, orders, and places, even exempt, in which the Office must be or is customarily said according to the usage and rite of the said Roman Church, excepting the aforementioned institution or custom exceeding two hundred years: decreeing that this Breviary, at no time, may be changed in whole or in part, nor may anything be added to or removed from it, and that all those bound by law or custom to recite or chant the Canonical Hours, according to the usage and rite of the Roman Church (the canonical laws having prescribed penalties for those who do not say the Divine Office daily), are expressly obliged henceforth, in perpetuity, to recite and chant the Hours, both of the day and of the night, in accordance with the prescription and form of this Roman Breviary, and that none of those upon whom this duty is formally imposed may fulfil it except in this form alone.

We therefore command all and each of the patriarchs, archbishops, bishops, abbots, and other prelates of the Churches to introduce this Breviary into their churches, monasteries, convents, orders, military orders, dioceses, and the aforementioned places, removing all other Breviaries, even those established by their private authority, which We have now suppressed and abolished; and it is enjoined upon them, as well as upon other priests, clerics, secular and regular, of either sex, even if belonging to military orders or exempt, who are bound to recite or chant the Office, to take care to recite or chant it, both in choir and outside, according to the form of this Breviary.

URBAN VIII, *SI QUID EST* (1634)[3]

If there is anything Divine among man's possessions that might excite the envy of the citizens of Heaven (could they ever be swayed by such a passion), this is undoubtedly the Most Holy

---

[3] Translation from *Sancta Liturgia*, November 7, 2005, https://sanctaliturgia. blogspot.com/2005/11/si-quid-est-english.html.

Sacrifice of the Mass, using which men, having before their eyes and taking into their hands the very Creator of Heaven and earth, experience, while still on earth, a certain anticipation of Heaven.

How keenly, then, must mortals strive to preserve and protect this inestimable privilege with all due worship and reverence and be ever on their guard lest their negligence offend the angels who vie with them in eager adoration!

Given this consideration, following in the footsteps of the Supreme Pontiffs, Our Predecessors, Pius V and Clement VIII, who undertook to review and restore most diligently the rite and prayers surrounding the celebration of this sacred Mystery, We have ordered that these be again examined and that if by chance anything, as often happens, has been corrupted over time, it shall be restored to its former standard.

Wherefore, just as We have recently achieved the reform of the Breviary for the greater splendour of the Divine Office, so also, following this example, We have ordered that the Missal be corrected to bestow greater beauty and luster upon the Divine Sacrifice.

And since it is highly becoming that the wings, as it were, of the liturgy which the priest, like the cherubim of the old Mystical Tabernacle, daily spreads over the true Mercy seat of the world, should be twofold and fashioned exactly in the same shape and form, We have entrusted this task to learned and pious men who have carried it out so carefully as to leave nothing to be desired.

The rubrics, which had been allowed to gradually degenerate from the old usage and rite, have been restored to their former pattern; those which did not seem to be easily intelligible to the readers have been more clearly stated; moreover, having compared the pertinent texts with the Vulgate edition of Holy Scripture, the differences which had crept into the Missal have been emended according to this standard and norm.

The competence of the revisers, however, is likely to bear little fruit, unless the skill and diligence of proficient printers measure up to it. We have, therefore, ordered Our dear son Andrew Brugiotto, director of Our printing establishment, to publish the Missal thus emended, and We allow it to be printed in the future outside the City, but only according to the standard now edited by Our printing establishment and after the printers have requested and obtained in writing the permission of Our most dear sons, the Inquisitors against heretical depravity, in those places where they are established and of the Ordinaries where there are no Inquisitors. Otherwise, if henceforth without this permission they dare to print the above-mentioned Missal or the booksellers dare to sell it, the printers and the booksellers established outside Our Ecclesiastical State shall incur excommunication *latae sententiae* from which, save on the point of death, they may not be absolved except by the Roman Pontiff. The printers and booksellers established in the City and other parts of the Ecclesiastical State shall incur the fine of five hundred gold ducats of the Treasury and forfeit unpardonably without any further declaration all their books and types which are to be devolved on the said Treasury. Nevertheless, We forbid and prohibit for all places and peoples under the same penalties the use of such Missals as might be printed and sold without the necessary permission.

Before granting this permission, the Inquisitors or the Ordinaries must very diligently compare the Missals to be printed, both before and after they have been printed, with the standard text revised by Our authority, and they must not allow anything to be added to or removed from it. In granting the original license, they must attest in their handwriting that, having made the comparison, the Missals are found to agree perfectly with the standard edition. This document must be printed always at the beginning or the end of every Missal.

If they behave otherwise, the Inquisitors shall incur, on that account, the penalty of being deprived of their office and of being debarred from obtaining it back and acquiring other offices in the future; the Ordinaries shall incur the penalty of suspension *a divinis* and of interdiction from entering the Church; and their Vicars shall be similarly deprived of their offices and benefices, they shall be debarred from obtaining these and other offices and benefices in the future and they shall incur excommunication, without any further declaration.

Wishing in Our Apostolic benignity to secure and protect from any loss all poor churches, clerics and ecclesiastics, printers, and booksellers, We allow them to keep, use, and sell respectively the Missals hitherto printed which they possess. Notwithstanding whatsoever license, indults, and privileges granted to the printers by Us or by the Roman Pontiffs, Our Predecessors, to print the Missal, which by these presents We expressly revoke and which

We wish to be revoked, as well as the constitutions, Apostolic ordinances, general and special, granted in whatever manner, contrary to the above prescriptions, confirmed and approved.

From all these ordinances, for this time only, We specially and expressly derogate, although particular, specific, and express mention is to be made of them and their whole tenor considering their tenor as expressed in these presents.

We wish that the same authority attaching to these presents if exhibited and shown be attributed to their copies, even printed ones, bearing the signature of a Notary Public, and vouched for by the seal of a Church dignitary.

Given in Rome at St. Mary Major's under the ring of the Fisherman, on the second day of September 1634, the twelfth year of Our Pontificate.

PIUS X, *DIVINO AFFLATU* (1911)[4]

The Psalms, composed under divine inspiration and collected in the Sacred Scriptures, have, from the very beginnings of the Church, been known not only to have marvelously fostered the piety of the faithful — who continually "offered to God the sacrifice of praise, that is, the fruit of lips confessing His name" (Heb. 13:15) — but also, following the custom already established in the Old Law, to have held a prominent place in the Sacred Liturgy and the Divine Office.

Thus, as Basil says, "the voice of the Church was born,"[5] and psalmody, "the daughter of her hymnody," as Our predecessor Urban VIII called it,[6] "is sung continually before the throne of God and the Lamb." It teaches men, especially those devoted to divine worship, in the judgment of Athanasius, "how God ought to be praised and with what words He may be fittingly confessed."[7] Augustine speaks beautifully to the point: "So that God may be well praised by man, God Himself praised Himself; and because He deigned to praise Himself, man found how he should praise Him."[8]

Moreover, there is a certain marvelous power in the Psalms to arouse in all minds a zeal for virtue. For although "all our

---

[4] Translation prepared for this publication.
[5] *Homil.* in Ps. 1, n. 2.
[6] Bulla *Divinam psalmodiam.*
[7] *Epist. ad Marcellinum in interpret. Psalm.*, n. 10.
[8] *In Psalm.* 144, n. 1.

Scripture, both Old and New, is divinely inspired and useful for teaching, as it is written . . . yet the Book of Psalms, as a kind of paradise containing the fruits of all the other books, gives forth songs and, moreover, presents its own particular ones to be sung with them."[9] Athanasius again states this, rightly adding: "It seems to me that for the one singing the Psalms, they are like a mirror, so that he may contemplate both himself and the movements of his own soul in them, and thus recite them with the appropriate feelings."[10] Thus Augustine, in his *Confessions*: "How much I wept at your hymns and songs, deeply moved by the sweet-sounding voices of your Church! Those voices flowed into my ears, and truth melted into my heart, and the feeling of devotion overflowed, and tears ran, and it was good for me with them."[11]

Indeed, who is not moved by those frequent passages in the Psalms where the immense majesty of God, His omnipotence, His ineffable justice, goodness, or mercy, and His other infinite praises are so exaltedly proclaimed? Who is not inspired with similar feelings by those acts of thanksgiving for benefits received from God, or by humble and confident prayers for benefits hoped for, or by the cries of the penitent soul for its sins? Who is not filled with admiration as the psalmist recounts the gifts of divine goodness bestowed upon the people of Israel and upon all mankind, and as he imparts the doctrines of heavenly wisdom? Finally, who is not inflamed with love by the diligently depicted image of Christ the Redeemer, "whose voice," as Augustine observed, is "heard in all the Psalms — now singing, now groaning, now rejoicing in hope, now sighing in reality"?[12]

Therefore, it was most wisely arranged from ancient times, by decrees of the Roman Pontiffs, by canons of Councils, and by monastic laws, that men of both the secular and regular clergy should sing or recite the entire Psalter each week. This law, handed down by the Fathers, was faithfully preserved by Our predecessors St. Pius V, Clement VIII, and Urban VIII in their revisions of the Roman Breviary. Hence, even now, the entire Psalter should be recited within the space of one week — were it not that, owing to changed circumstances, such recitation is frequently impeded.

---

[9] *Epist. ad Marcell.* cit., n. 2.
[10] Op. cit., n. 12.
[11] Lib. IX, cap. 6.
[12] *In Psalm.* 42, n. 1.

As time went on, the number of those among the faithful whom the Church, after their mortal life, was accustomed to enroll among the heavenly citizens and to propose to the Christian people as patrons and guides for living, saw continual increase. In their honor, Offices of the Saints gradually began to multiply, so that it almost came about that the Offices of Sundays and weekdays fell silent, and thus not a few Psalms were neglected, which, as Ambrose says, are, like the others, "the blessing of the people, the praise of God, the praise of the people, the applause of all, the speech of all, the voice of the Church, the melodious confession of faith, the devotion full of authority, the joy of liberty, the shout of gladness, the echo of joy."[13] More than once have serious complaints been made by prudent and pious men about such omissions, not only because so many aids for praising the Lord and for expressing the innermost feelings of the soul to Him were thus withdrawn from sacred ministers, but also because that desirable variety in prayer, so very helpful to our weakness for praying worthily, attentively, and devoutly, was lacking. For, as Basil observes, "in sameness the mind often grows sluggish, I know not how, and is present yet absent; but when psalmody and singing are varied and changed each hour, desire is renewed and attention restored."[14]

It is therefore not surprising that many bishops from various parts of the world brought their wishes on this matter to the Apostolic See, especially at the Vatican Council, when, among other things, they requested that, as far as possible, the ancient custom of reciting the whole Psalter each week be restored, but in such a way that no greater burden be placed on the clergy, already laboring more heavily in the vineyard of sacred ministry due to the diminished number of workers. To these requests and wishes — which were also Ours before We assumed the Pontificate — and to the prayers subsequently offered by other venerable brothers and pious men, We have deemed it right to accede, but with caution, lest, on the one hand, by requiring the entire Psalter to be recited within a week, something be lost from the cult of the Saints, or, on the other hand, the burden of the Divine Office become more onerous for the clergy, rather than more manageable.

---

[13] *Enarrat. in Ps.* 1, n. 9.
[14] *Regulae fusius tractatae*, interrog. 37, n. 5.

Therefore, after humbly imploring the Father of lights and
gathering the suffrages of holy prayers for this very purpose,
following in the footsteps of Our predecessors, We chose several
learned and industrious men, to whom We entrusted the task of
finding, by shared counsel and study, a definite way to achieve
this goal that would meet Our wishes. They, faithfully carrying
out the task entrusted to them, developed a new arrangement of
the Psalter; and when the Cardinals of the Holy Roman Church
responsible for sacred rites had carefully considered and approved
it, We, finding it very much in accord with Our mind, ratified it
in all respects — that is, regarding the order and distribution of
the Psalms, the Antiphons, Versicles, Hymns, with their Rubrics
and Rules — and ordered its authentic edition to be prepared and
published by Our Vatican Press.

Since the arrangement of the Psalter is closely connected with
the entire Divine Office and Liturgy, it is clear to all that by these
decrees We have taken the first step toward the emendation of
the Roman Breviary and Missal; but for this purpose, We will
soon establish a special Council or Commission of learned men.
Meanwhile, now that the occasion presents itself, We have decided
that some things should be renewed at present, as prescribed
in the appropriate Rubrics: first, that in the recitation of the
Divine Office, the proper honor due to the appointed readings
from Sacred Scripture with their responsories occurring in the
season should be restored by more frequent use; then, that in
the sacred Liturgy of the Mass, the most ancient Masses of the
Sundays throughout the year and of the weekdays, especially in
Lent, should recover their rightful place.

Therefore, by the authority of these letters, We first of all
abolish the arrangement of the Psalter as it exists today in the
Roman Breviary and completely forbid its use from the first of
January in the year 1913. From that day, in all churches of secular
and regular clergy, in monasteries, orders, congregations, and
religious institutes, by all and each who, by office or custom,
recite the canonical Hours according to the Roman Breviary, as
edited by St. Pius V and revised by Clement VIII, Urban VIII,
and Leo XIII, the new order of the Psalter, as We have approved
it with its Rules and Rubrics and decreed to be published by the
Vatican Press, must be religiously observed. At the same time,
We warn that the penalties established in law will be incurred by

those who fail in their duty of daily recitation of the canonical Hours; and they should know that they will not fulfill so grave an obligation unless they use this Our disposition of the Psalter.

Therefore, We command all Patriarchs, Archbishops, Bishops, Abbots, and other prelates of churches — not excepting even the Cardinal Archpriests of the patriarchal basilicas of the City — that in each one's diocese, church, or monastery, the Psalter with its Rules and Rubrics, as We have arranged it, be introduced at the appointed time; and We strictly order that this Psalter and its Rules and Rubrics be inviolably applied and observed by all others as well, whoever is bound by the obligation of reciting or singing the canonical Hours. Meanwhile, any chapter itself, provided that the majority of its members so wish, may lawfully adopt the new order of the Psalter immediately after its publication.

We proclaim, declare, sanction, and decree that these Our letters are and shall always be valid and effective, notwithstanding apostolic constitutions and ordinances, general or special, and everything else whatsoever to the contrary. Therefore, let no one infringe this page of Our abolition, revocation, permission, command, precept, statute, indult, mandate, and will, or dare to contravene it with rash boldness. If anyone should presume to attempt this, let him know that he will incur the indignation of Almighty God and of the blessed Apostles Peter and Paul.

Given at Rome, at St. Peter's, in the year of the Lord's Incarnation 1911, on the Kalends of November, on the Feast of All Saints, in the ninth year of Our Pontificate.

FURTHER READING

Bugnini, Annibale. *The Reform of the Liturgy, 1948–1975*. Liturgical Press, 1990.

——. "For a General Reform." *Restore the '54*, November 16, 2022. https://cdn.restorethe54.com/media/pdf/bugnini-for-a-general-liturgical-reform-1949.pdf

Bux, Nicola, Peter Gumpel, and Alexandra von Teuffenbach. *Pio XII E Il Concilio (Pius XII and the Council)*. Cantagalli Publishers, 2012.

Carusi, Stephano. "The Reform of Holy Week in the Years 1951–1956." *Rorate Caeli*, March 25, 2018. https://rorate-caeli.blogspot.com/2015/04/the-reform-of-holy-week-in-years-1951.html.

Chiron, Yves. *Annibale Bugnini: Reformer of the Liturgy*. Angelico Press, 2018.

Davies, Michael. "The Destruction of the Traditional Roman Rite." *Virgo Sacrata*, August 9, 2022. www.virgosacrata.com/traditional-roman-rite-destruction.html.

DiPippo, Gregory. "Compendium of the 1955 Holy Week Revisions of Pius XII." A series in many parts, published over many years at *New Liturgical Movement*. A table of contents is given in the final installment: "Compendium of the 1955 Holy Week Revisions of Pius XII: Part 10 — Conclusion," www.newliturgicalmovement.org/2023/03/compendium-of-1955-holy-week-revisions.html.

Eger, Gerhard. "Pre-'62 General Rubrics of the Roman Missal." *Canticum Salomonis*, July 17, 2020. https://sicutincensum.wordpress.com/2020/07/17/pre-62-general-rubrics-of-the-roman-missal/.

Giampietro, Nicola. *The Development of the Liturgical Reform: As Seen by Cardinal Ferdinando Antonelli from 1948 to 1970*. Roman Catholic Books, 2009.

Hesse, Gregory. "Mass of 1962 vs the Mass of Pope St. Pius V." *Odysee*, November 26, 2013. https://odysee.com/@defeatmodernism:c/fr.-hesse-mass-of-1962-vs-the-mass-of:a.

Kwasniewski, Peter. *The Once and Future Roman Rite: Returning to the Traditional Latin Liturgy after Seventy Years of Exile*. TAN Books, 2022.

——. "Just How Different Are the Pre-1955, 1962, and 1969 Calendars Around Christmas and Epiphany?" *Rorate Caeli*, December 27, 2024. https://rorate-caeli.blogspot.com/2024/12/just-how-different-are-pre-1955-1962.html.

——. "Why Restoring the Roman Rite to its Fullness is not 'Traddy Antiquarianism.'" *New Liturgical Movement*, August 12, 2019. www.

newliturgicalmovement.org/2019/08/why-restoring-roman-rite-to-its.html.

Reid, Alcuin. *The Organic Development of the Liturgy*. Ignatius Press, 2005.

Restore the '54. "Comparisons." *Restore the '54*, September 9, 2022. www.restorethe54.com/comparisons.

The Rad Trad. "The Legality of the Old Rite." October 25, 2018. https://theradtrad.blogspot.com/2018/10/the-legality-of-old-rite.html.

BIBLIOGRAPHY

In addition to works listed above in Further Reading:

Acta Apostolicae Sedis. Vol. 39. Libreria Editrice Vaticana, 1947.

"Anglophone Missals of the 'Interim Rite' 1964–1969: I." *The Saint Bede Studio,* December 16, 2014. https://saintbedestudio.blogspot. com/2014/12/anglophone-missals-of-interim-rite-1964.html.

Beal, John. *New Commentary on the Code of Canon Law.* Paulist Press, 2000.

Braga, Carlo. "Fr Carlo Braga on the 1955 Holy Week Reform." *New Liturgical Movement.* June 1–4, 2022.

Brill, Patrick John. *The Great Sacred Music Reform of Pope St. Pius X.* Os Justi Press, 2024.

Bugnini, Annibale. *The Simplification of the Rubrics.* Doyle and Finegan, 1955.

Butler, Thomas. *The Truths of the Catholic Religion: Proved from Scripture Alone.* C. Dolman, 1841.

Byrne, Carol. "Fourteen Other Feast Days Abolished." Tradition in Action, September 16, 2019. https://traditioninaction.org/HotTopics/f175_Dialogue_91.htm.

Cekada, Anthony. "The Nine vs. Lefebvre: We Resist You to Your Face." 2008. www.traditionalmass.org/images/articles/NineVLefebvre.pdf.

Code of Canon Law. Accessed March 4, 2025. Libreria Editrice Vaticana. www.vatican.va/archive/cod-iuris-canonici/cic_index_en.html.

Consilium. "*Inter Oecumenici* Instruction on Implementing Liturgical Norms." *Adoremus,* September 26, 1964. https://adoremus.org/1964/09/inter-oecumenici/.

Coomaraswamy, Rama. *The Destruction of the Christian Tradition.* World Wisdom, 2006.

"The Coronation of Pope Leo XIII." *The Catholic World 27,* no. 158 (1878): 280–85. https://name.umdl.umich.edu/bac8387.0027.158.

de la Franquerie, Maquis. *L'infaillibilité pontificale: le Syllabus, la condamnation du modernisme et la crise actuelle de l'Église. Conférences.* 2nd ed. Diffusion de la pensée française, 1974.

DiPippo, Gregory. "Bad Scholarship on the Easter Vigil." *New Liturgical Movement,* May 14, 2020. www.newliturgicalmovement.org/2020/05/bad-scholarship-on-easter-vigil.html.

——. "The Legal Achievement of *Summorum Pontificum*." *New Liturgical Movement,* July 5, 2017.

——. "What Really Happened to the Sequences?" *New Liturgical Movement,* May 5, 2022.

Dolan, Daniel L. "The Pius X and John XXIII Missals Compared." *traditionalmass.org.* Accessed April 1, 2025. www.traditionalmass.org/articles/article.php?id=18.

Fitzgerald, William. "The Liturgical Movement from Pope St. Pius X to Pope Francis: An Evaluation." Mount St. Mary's Seminary & School of Theology. YouTube, May 12, 2016. www.youtube.com/watch?v= K9dorKlt_bA.

Fortescue, Adrian. *The Ceremonies of the Roman Rite Described.* Burns, Oates & Washbourne, 1920.

——. *The Mass: A Study of the Roman Liturgy.* Longmans, Green & Co., 1914.

"Good Friday (Repost)." *The Rad Trad,* April 3, 2015. https://theradtrad. blogspot.com/2015/04/good-friday-repost.html.

Hand Missal History. https://handmissalhistory.com/.

Hesse, Gregory. "Canon Lawyer on the Validity Invalidity of the Novus Ordo Sacraments." Internet Archive, archived June 30, 2016, at https:// archive.org/details/CanonLawyerOnTheValidityInvalidityOfThe NovusOrdoSacraments.

International Congress of Pastoral Liturgy. *The Assisi Papers: Proceedings of the First International Congress of Pastoral Liturgy, Assisi-Rome, September 18-22, 1956.* Literary Licensing, 2011.

Jenkins, William, SSPV. "Why Does SSPX Use the 1962 Missal?" www. youtube.com/watch?v=h_esB7bqioU.

Jungmann, Josef A. *The Mass of the Roman Rite: Its Origins and Development (Missarum Sollemnia).* Translated by Francis A. Brunner. Benziger, 1951.

Kenney, Keith. "Divino Afflatu (English)." Blogspot, November 10, 2005. https://sanctaliturgia.blogspot.com/2005/11/divino-afflatu-english.html.

King, Archdale A. *Liturgy of the Roman Church.* Bruce Publishing Co., 1957.

Kwasniewski, Peter. *Bound by Truth: Authority, Obedience, Tradition, and the Common Good.* Angelico Press, 2023.

——. *Close the Workshop: Why the Old Mass Isn't Broken and the New Mass Can't Be Fixed.* Angelico Press, 2025.

——. "Does a Priest Need Permission to Offer the Traditional Latin Mass?" *Tradition and Sanity Substack,* April 3, 2025.

——. "The Excision of the Institution Narratives from Pius XII's Holy Week." *New Liturgical Movement.* July 8, 2024.

——. "The Homily Is Not Part of the Liturgy." *The Remnant.* January 15, 2021. https://remnantnewspaper.com/web/index.php/fetzen-fliegen/ item/5234-the-homily-is-not-part-of-the-liturgy.

——. *Ministers of Christ: Recovering the Roles of Clergy and Laity in an Age of Confusion.* Crisis Publications, 2021.

——. "Minutes from the Commission of Cardinals That Advised John Paul II to Lift Restrictions on the Old Missal." *New Liturgical Movement,* January 9, 2023.

——. "Objections and Replies on *Pastor Aeternus*." In *Bound by Truth: Authority, Obedience, Tradition, and the Common Good*, 30–38. Angelico Press, 2023.

——. "On the Insertion of St Joseph's Name into the Roman Canon." *New Liturgical Movement*, December 23, 2019.

——. "The Pope's Boundedness to Tradition as a Legislative Limit." In *From Benedict's Peace to Francis's War: Catholics Respond to the Motu Proprio "Traditionis Custodes" on the Latin Mass*, ed. idem, 222–47. Angelico Press, 2021.

——, ed. *A Reader in Catholic Social Teaching from* Syllabus Errorum *to* Deus Caritas Est. Cluny Media, 2017.

——. *Turned Around: Replying to Common Objections Against the Traditional Latin Mass*. TAN Books, 2024.

Lefebvre, Marcel. "Lefebvre Ridgefield 1982 '83 Talk to Seminarians." Typescript. https://archive.org/details/LefebvreRidgefield8283A/.

——. "Letter to American Friends & Benefactors" (28 April 28, 1983). Cited in Nicholas Mary, "Matters Arising: Why Does the Society Use the Missal of 1962?" Great Britain Society of Saint Pius X. Accessed April 7, 2025. https://fsspx.uk/en/matters-arising-why-does-society -use-missal-1962-35683.

"The Letter of 'The Nine' to Archbishop Lefebvre." March 25, 1983. www. traditionalmass.org/images/articles/NineLetter.pdf.

Morlin, Nicholas. "Faith of Our Fathers: Traditional Catholic Customs, Privileges, and Indults granted to the Catholic Church in Australia." *Restore the '54*, January 4, 2024. https://cdn.restorethe54.com/media/ pdf/faith-of-our-fathers.pdf.

——. *Manuale Sacrarum Caeremoniarum: Editio Simplex*. Lulu Press, 2023.

——. *A Sacristan's Guide to the Traditional Roman Rite*. Lulu Press, 2022.

Ostrowski, Jeff. "'Pope Pius XII Psalter': How Different Was It?" Corpus Christi Watershed, July 22, 2020. www.ccwatershed.org/2020/07/21/ pius-xii-psalter-just-how-different-was-it/.

Pecklers, Keith F. *The Living Language of Christian Worship*. Liturgical Press, 2003.

Petit, Vincent. *Église et Nation*. Presses universitaires de Rennes, 2010. https://doi.org/10.4000/books.pur.110168.

Pius V. *Quo Primum*. Translated by John Warrington. New Advent, July 14, 1570. www.newadvent.org/library/docs_pio5qp.htm.

Pius XI. *Quas Primas*. Libreria Editrice Vaticana. December 11, 1925. www. vatican.va/content/pius-xi/en/encyclicals/documents/hf_p-xi_enc_ 11121925_quas-primas.html.

"Questions for the Rector | Ep. 31: Bishop Richard N. Williamson." MHT Seminary. YouTube, February 26, 2025. www.youtube.com/watch?v= 57dUrYBs964&ab_ channel=MHTSeminary.

Quoëx, Franck Marie. "The Traditional Mass: the Sun of our Lives." *Rorate Caeli*, January 28, 2007. https://rorate-caeli.blogspot.com/2007/01/traditional-mass-sun-of-our-lives.html.

Reid, Alcuin. "Holy Week Reforms Revisited—Some New Material and Paths for Further Study." In *Liturgy in the Twenty-First Century: Contemporary Issues and Perspectives*, ed. idem, 234–59. Bloomsbury T&T Clark, 2016.

Rivoire, Réginald-Marie. *Does "Traditionis Custodes" Pass the Juridical Rationality Test? A Canonical-Theological Study*. Os Justi Press, 2022.

Roman Missal. Catholic Book Publishing Co., 1964.

Sacred Congregation for Rites. *De Musica Sacra et Sacra Liturgia*—Instruction on Sacred Music and Sacred Liturgy. *Adoremus*, September 3, 1958. https://adoremus.org/1958/09/instruction-on-sacred-music/.

Sacred Congregation of the Council. Decree on Frequent & Daily Reception of Holy Communion. EWTN, December 20, 1905. www.ewtn.com/catholicism/library/decree-on-frequent-daily-reception-of-holy-communion-2174.

Shaw, Joseph, ed. *The Case for Liturgical Restoration*. Angelico Press, 2019.

Sonnen, John Paul. "The First Permanent Altar Facing the People in the United States." *Liturgical Arts Journal*, December 3, 2024. www.liturgicalartsjournal.com/2024/12/the-first-permanent-altar-facing-people.html.

Tribe, Shawn. "The Ceremonies of Good Friday in the Papal Chapel and St. Peter's as Described in 1839." *Liturgical Arts Journal*, April 15, 2022. www.liturgicalartsjournal.com/2022/04/the-ceremonies-of-good-friday-in-papal.html.

——. "The History and Forms of the Christian Altar: The Twentieth Century to Present." *Liturgical Arts Journal*, May 5, 2023. www.liturgicalartsjournal.com/2023/05/the-history-and-forms-of-christian.html.

Urban VIII. *Si Quid Est*. English translation. *Sancta Liturgia*, September 2, 1634. https://sanctaliturgia.blogspot.com/2005/11/si-quid-est-english.html.

van der Stappen, Josephus F. *Sacra Liturgia*. H. Dessain, 1904.

"Why Does SSPX Use the 1962 Missal?" *What Catholics Believe*. YouTube, October 28, 2023. www.youtube.com/watch?v=h_esB7bqioU&ab_channel=WhatCatholicsBelieve-Highlights.

www.ingramcontent.com/pod-product-compliance
Lightning Source LLC
Chambersburg PA
CBHW021636120626
46545CB00002B/570